BELIEVERS IN BUSINESS

STORIES FROM THE SERVICEMASTER FAMILY

As told to
Elyse Fitzpatrick

Believers in Business: Stories from the ServiceMaster Family
Copyright ©2001 by ServiceMaster Clean

Packaged by Pine Hill Graphics

All rights reserved

ISBN 0-9714103-1-3

Unless otherwise noted, quotations at the beginning of each chapter are taken from *The Lord Is My Counsel: A Businessman's Personal Experiences with the Bible* by Marion E. Wade with Glenn D. Kittler.

Believers in Business was funded exclusively by ServiceMaster Clean.

Printed in the United States of America.

DEDICATION

To every member of the ServiceMaster Clean family,
who gets it done every day,
and to Marion E. Wade,
whose vision still lights their path.

CONTENTS

———

ACKNOWLEDGMENTS

An undertaking of this sort, involving so many people, would be impossible without the help and cooperation of others. I want to thank Mike and Jinny Isakson for having the vision for this project and allowing me the glad privilege of hearing and reflecting on these stories. Mimi Blanton needs special recognition, since this project confronted her with trying to be chief counsel for ServiceMaster while also kindly engaging in trivial pursuits for me. Jim Wassell and others at the home office offered much help, as well. This entire project was funded by ServiceMaster Clean in an effort to honor the franchisees that have made our business what it is today.

I interviewed a number of people whose stories did not end up in the book. Though their stories aren't here, it's very clear that their lives are a testimony that continues to impact many people. Your stories live on in the lives of your employees and everyone else in your sphere of influence—that's what is most important. Thank you for affording me the great joy of hearing your narrative.

Gerry and Barbara Farrelly have been kind benefactors to our family through the years: we wouldn't have known about ServiceMaster or Marion Wade aside from your generosity; thank you.

Steve Miller, my editor from Harvest House, who helped refine these stories into a clear testimony to Marion E. Wade's legacy. My daughter, Jessica Thompson, transcribed all the tapes from the interviews. My mother, Rosemary Buerger, acted as a proofreader and Encourager General.

The ones who need the most thanks, however, are the members of my family, particularly my husband, Phil, who had to put up with "less than sumptuous" dinners until this project was completed. Phil, you've been a great help and, like so many others I've had the chance to get to know, you're the embodiment of the ServiceMaster Clean philosophy. Our children—James, Jessica and Cody, Joel and Ruth—and grandchildren Wesley and Hayden have waited patiently for Mimi to be ready to go play again. Thank you.

SERVICEMASTER'S
FOUR CORPORATE OBJECTIVES

To honor God in all we do
To help people develop
To pursue excellence
To grow profitably

INTRODUCTION:
A Most Remarkable Family

The muted hues and stark shadows stretched gracefully across the Arizona desert as my husband, Phil, and I sat down to dinner with Mike and Jinny Isakson. During the next few hours, as we interacted with others around the table and enjoyed a sumptuous meal, I began to understand what we were doing there. With his childlike enthusiasm and great powers of persuasion, Mike began to unfold before us the vision that was captivating him. His bright dream soon captivated us as well.

"Think of the wonderful people in this organization," he said fervently. "Think of the founders, their sacrifice, what they've accomplished. ServiceMaster is just bursting with fantastic stories! How can we preserve them?" he wondered. "How can we honor the franchisees? There they are, working in the trenches—how can I communicate my admiration for what they do every day? These stories have got to be written down! What can we do to make that happen?"

What you now hold in your hands is the fruit of the conversation we had, as we gazed across the desert floor in Scottsdale, Arizona in March 2000. As I sat there, agreeing with Mike about the quality of the ServiceMaster family that I was already acquainted with, I couldn't have foreseen how this project would shape and impact me.

Over the last year, I've been splendidly enlightened. I've had the privilege to get to know former and present franchisees and distributors. I've asked tough questions; I've pushed for the "real story." Without any hyperbole, I can honestly say that many times I would finish an interview and then just shake my head in wonder. Were there really so many people who sacrificed for seemingly insignificant employees, who loved honesty more than money, who worked their whole lives just to make a place for their children? I had been familiar with some of the Marion E. Wade and Ken Hansen stories, but were their beliefs still so alive even now? Were there really people who had a standard of ethics that meant more to them than profit margins? This book presents only a fraction of what I've been privileged to learn, a small portion of how I've been illuminated.

My hope is that I've been able to portray—before the watching, cynical, blase business world—what's really going on here in our family. As you read these stories, you might have bouts of skepticism, wondering if these people are for real. You might be tempted to say, "This is a nice little piece of propaganda." All I can do is tell you that I've merely written down the stories the way they were told to me. These people are real people; I haven't embellished their stories or tried to make their lives appear better than they are. If their stories seem too good to be true, it might be because I haven't been able to convincingly communicate the truth of their integrity, bravery, and compassion. Because this book had to end at some point, we couldn't include everyone in the company, although there are thousands of other stories that belong here as well.

WHAT *ONE* WORD?

One key question I asked during the interviews was this: "Each business has a unique character that is all its own. What *one word* would you use to describe the character of your business? How does your business reflect that character?"

What you'll find in this book are the answers to that question. But first, I'd like to answer it based on all the people I had the privilege of meeting. What *one word* would I use to describe the character of the ServiceMaster Clean family? *Remarkable.* That's the word that kept coming up in my mind, as I finished interviews, read over transcripts, or reviewed a story. Again and again I've sat in awe and thought, *Remarkable.* These people are unusual, exceptional, extraordinary, uncommon, rare. The ServiceMaster Clean family is simply, in a word, *remarkable.*

My involvement with ServiceMaster began humbly when my husband took a job cleaning carpets for Gerry Farrelly in 1976. We were young, we had little children, we needed money. It was a job. What seemed to Phil and me like a desperation move at the time, turned into an opportunity that has since shaped the direction of our lives and our children's lives.

Over the last 25 years ServiceMaster has become more to us than merely a way to pay our bills. ServiceMaster is a philosophy. It's a philosophy of ethics, honesty, hard work, love, and sacrifice. It's a philosophy of putting others first. It's unabashedly old-fashioned. It's so old-fashioned, in fact, that it finds its genesis in the Ancient Truth.

The ServiceMaster philosophy is not something these people might fake for an interview, because, as Phil and I have experienced, the pressures to conform, to acquiesce to the gods of this world, are too powerful to resist if not securely anchored in the soul. What I've learned, what's truly remarkable, is that the people who've made ServiceMaster their life's vocation really do believe this philosophy. Why? What makes this business family so different?

MARION E. WADE'S STORY

Marion E. Wade prayed for this company. Whether or not you are a person who unashamedly believes in prayer like I do, everyone has to admit that what's been built is a testimony to Marion's faith. He prayed that he would have a business that would impact the corporate world. He prayed that this company would be something that he could present to God. "I wanted men working with me who would know what the Lord had done and was doing," he wrote, "because with such men I knew that, as the Lord was receiving me into His glory, I would be able to tell Him that His company was still working for Him."

Perhaps Marion was naive, but contemplate for a moment what he's accomplished. "What would happen," he wondered, "if a business was totally dedicated to honoring God in the marketplace?" In my own personal life, I've been encouraged as I've seen how much of an impact one man's simple faith has had. Who could count the lives that have been changed because of his vision?

What you hold in your hands is a testimony to the faith of Marion E. Wade and thousands of others who have followed in his footsteps. These people are people who have refused to take the easy road; who have sought to build a team so that others could develop and prosper; who have longed to deliver excellent service and who have ultimately profited because of it. Marion Wade's personal development as a businessman brought him far more prosperity and goodwill than he would have ever known if he had made the "big leagues." Today ServiceMaster employs more than 50,000 people, manages approximately 190,000 others, and has a system-wide revenue of $7.8 billion serving 10.5 million customers in 40 countries.

THE LIGHT BEGAN TO DAWN

Even though the sky was darkening as our dinner conversation came to a close that night in the Arizona desert, Mike Isakson had communicated a bright vision to Phil and me, and now it's here for you to see. But it is more than just a light to be examined and probed. It is a light that beckons to be followed.

How would you answer the question about the character of your business? What will be said about your life, about your collective business ethic? Will future generations look back with wonder at the contribution that you've made to your family, your community, your culture? It's my prayer that this book will not only save for posterity the truth about this very unique company, but that it will also motivate each one of us, whether or not we're in the ServiceMaster family, to live lives that count, to stand for something beyond ourselves, to be *truly remarkable.*

"THEM THAT HONOR ME, I WILL HONOR"

The Story of George Meyer, Jr.

"We are here to take care of each other.
We are to care."

Marion E. Wade[1]

George Meyer, Jr. had high hopes in the early 1950s when Art Melvin, a man he had become acquainted with through church, told him and his friend "Bud" Waardenburg about the developing prospects in the rug-cleaning business.

George remembers their first experiences with Art: "He put stars in our eyes. He was the first person to tell us that one day, possibly in the near future, everyone would have wall-to-wall carpeting. That was very hard for us to believe because in Florida, where we were living, everyone had either concrete or terrazzo floors and very little wall-to-wall carpeting. But Art sold us on that fact."

As George and Bud thought and prayed about the prospect that was available to them in a fledgling, new enterprise called ServiceMaster, they decided to take the risk. In 1955, ServiceMaster Services, Inc. opened its doors for business.

In 1965, after only ten years of operation, their business received the first Marion E. Wade Award ever given, and in 1984, George bought out Bud's interest in the business. Although by anyone's standards George is a very successful businessman today, having sold and supervised 175 franchisees in Florida and Georgia as a distributor, his life was not always so prosperous.

His father, George, Sr., had emigrated to America from Holland when he was 16. He met and married George's mother, Anna, who was also Dutch and soon there were ten children to feed and clothe. "It wasn't easy for my dad to care for ten children, especially in the late 1920s," George said. "My father wasn't home much because he was always working. Very early on I learned that I needed to do things for myself if I was ever going to get ahead in life. I was an entrepreneur very early."

YOUNG ENTREPRENEURIAL EXPERIENCE

At the age of nine George went to his father and said, "Pop, I really need a bicycle." His father looked down into his eyes and, with a heavy Dutch accent, asked him, "Well, and what for?" "Dad," little George answered, "if I had a bike I could sell newspapers, and I could do a lot of things. I could make money." "If *you* want a bike, *you* see that you get one," was his father's stern reply.

Without much help and little encouragement, George, Jr. discovered that by selling magazine subscriptions door to door he could earn "points" that would eventually enable him to purchase the bike he wanted. After three months of persistent selling, he had sold enough subscriptions of *Saturday Evening Post* and *Ladies' Home Journal* to buy a bicycle for himself and also a wind-up watch for his sister. George's entrepreneurial desire was force-fed by his father's advice, "It is better to be a small businessman than a big workman."

A resolute work ethic was indelibly imprinted on George's heart during his childhood years, as George recalls. "My father taught me that if I could own my own business, I could determine my own destiny—and self-determination was an opportunity that might not be available to me if I were working in a large corporation."

After spending some time in military service and in a franchise food business, George found a home in ServiceMaster. Then once he met Marion Wade, he was more sure of the rightness of his commitment because he discovered ServiceMaster was a company founded on Christian principles.

"My parents brought us up to be very devout," George confessed. "They taught us that the most important thing in life was our relationship with Jesus Christ. Marion Wade was a man who believed that also. He was a tremendous witness to his beliefs." George relished the idea of being involved with a national company that held the same beliefs he did. "I felt like it was a great opportunity to be involved in something that we could someday be very, very proud of."

Early on, George decided that the core beliefs of the founders would be the foundation upon which his business was built as well. "Every new person that comes into our business learns what the four corporate objectives mean. We always give them an opportunity to discuss them with us. It's part of the employment interview," George stated. "New employees need to commit themselves to be a part of that foundation. It is the bedrock of our company, and we talk about it whenever we have an opportunity. We will do that as long as I am part of the company," he vowed. "It's unfair to bring a new employee into the organization who doesn't understand how important the corporate objectives are to us. I tell them that these objectives are probably something that they've never encountered before. But Scripture says, 'Them that honor Me, I will honor.' That is a promise, and I believe God honors that and helps us be successful in our business."

As Plain as Apple Pie

George cherishes the memories of his experiences with both Marion Wade and Ken Hansen. He recalls them as being humble, friendly men, "just as plain as apple pie and ice cream. They were just wonderful people."

One of those memories has to do with the time that George and Denis Horsfall had attended the first Building Service Engineer Training Program in Chicago. George and Denis were staying at the Lakeshore Club. Marion inquired as to where they were staying, and then he and his wife Lillian invited them to stay in their home.

"I remember that he had a wonderful library and den, and we felt like we were really special to be able to sit there with him. Marion said to us, 'Now guys, make use of this while you are here. It is all yours, just make use of it.' They were so very kind," George remembers. "A day or two later when the Wades had to leave town they told us, 'You guys take the key and stay here until you are ready to go home.' It was just as if he had known us for a thousand years. He was just wonderful, and we had a lot of fun with him and his wife."

"Then Ken Hansen provided us with a little Volkswagen automobile to drive, and the crowning joy of that trip was that Ken and his wife, Jean, invited Denis and I into their home for Thanksgiving dinner. We had a wonderful time with their family, and it is one of the greatest memories that I have."

George Meyer, Jr. has seen the fulfillment of Marion Wade's dream. When Marion Wade was trying to convince Ken Hansen to come into the business Marion had said,

"Ken, think about what can be done in the marketplace if we honor God in all we do." George has thought about that, too, and he's seen firsthand what can happen.

AN INTENTIONAL GENEROSITY

Coming from a background of grinding poverty with the prospect of never-ending toil, coupled with the tragedy of losing his mother when he was just 17, one might suppose that George would have ended up a modern-day Ebenezer Scrooge. But just the opposite is true. His earnest and compelling faith in God and care for others has kept him far from the self-serving greediness that marks so many businessmen today. You see, to George success isn't measured by the bottom-line alone. Although he's always held to Ken Hansen's philosophy of frugality in business, he believes that success is not measured by a number on a bank statement but by a different number: that number being the lives that he has touched and changed for good. For George, that isn't some pious platitude—it's a core belief that has reached all the way into his wallet.

In 1992 George and his managers decided that they had to do something to prove that they really believed in the four corporate objectives. "How can we demonstrate our conviction we should honor God in all we do and commit ourselves to developing people? Further," they wondered, "how can we work that out in a concrete manner especially for minorities?" In response to those self-imposed questions, they allocated $75,000 of their own funds that year to sponsor five minorities in new franchise opportunities, or as they called it, "incubator programs." Their goal was to enable people who had a strong desire but lacked the financial resources and business savvy to be successful as a small business owner.

The programs were called "incubator programs" for all the obvious reasons: they looked at each new owner as a "premie"—a baby that would require spoon-feeding and constant care. They knew that they would have to care for those businesses and, in a sense, parent them until they were able to care for themselves. That was in 1992, and today, two of the five "premie" businesses have grown up to successful maturity—one with very significant revenues.

Why would George Meyer take time from his own business to help build others? Because he has always had a burning desire to demonstrate his gratefulness to the God who has chosen him and given him so much. For many people, the opportunity brought by money and support "makes all the difference. Those two people are examples of what can happen if we care about others."

WE ARE HERE TO SERVE

George's manner of interviewing prospective employees may seem to some to be very exacting, but it's made for great relationships in his business. He's concerned that the people who give their time to him "fit well" into his organization. And although he has constantly been careful to make his businesses profitable, he's also worked hard to care for his employees.

"We have always been sensitive to the people that work for us. For instance, I have one employee who has worked for me for 42 years and several others who have been with me for 25 or more years. One of the things we are very careful to point out to our employees is that we are here to serve other people. In the position that I'm in as a distributor, I believe that I'm not a true representative of ServiceMaster if I don't put the other person first."

One evening George received a call from Debra, the wife of one of the franchise owners that he had brought into the business.

"My husband was just killed in a motorcycle accident. What am I going to do?" she sobbed. At the time her situation certainly did look bleak. She earned only a small amount of money at her job in a bank and had no idea how to run her husband's business or how she was going to care for her young family. But George and his staff cared for her and picked up the burden that, at that time, was more than Debra could bear. For the first week after her bereavement someone from the business traversed the 200-mile distance every day to comfort and encourage her. As time went on, the ServiceMaster family from George Meyer's office began to teach her how to run a service business—how to manage the finances, do the sales, and hire and train employees. Today, Debra is remarried and is a successful businesswoman.

What makes George a ServiceMaster Clean success story? A prime example is the help he offered to Debra— helping her to get established and save her husband's business, not to mention her family's home. Debra will never forget the years that George and his staff spent with her, and more importantly, neither will he. The truth about him is that, although these stories seem outstanding to others, to a humble man like George Meyer, they are just how one should live. At a time when employers are moaning about the difficulty in finding and retaining good employees, George Meyer has people on his staff who have been with him for decades.

What is the secret to his success as an employer...as a businessman? Caring. In this day when the word *caring* has become just another marketing tool to bilk the public, George believes in something more than shallow service. He sincerely believes that it is his primary vocation to help others develop and grow. He doesn't do this to gain any monetary advantage, nor for any kudos that will quickly fade from view. He orders all his life in this way because he believes that honoring God means that you care for others before you care for yourself. He genuinely believes that, as Marion Wade said, "The commandment to put others first applies to the business world as well as everywhere else."[2]

Bev Payne, an employee who has been with George for over 22 years, came into the business as a single mother with two young children. She had worked for him in a part-time capacity but because of changes in her home situation, she needed more hours.

"At the time I had 52 franchisees, and I really needed help working with the franchise group. I interviewed her about this job, and she said, 'I don't know anything about it, but I sure would like to have the opportunity.'" That was two decades ago and now, as George nears retirement, Bev is in position to assume the business and is chief operating officer.

"Talk about a person who has grown. I will never forget the first time I asked her to speak to franchisees. I felt so sorry for her. Her whole face just quivered," George tenderly recalls. "She couldn't get the words out. She has always said that it was simply because we gave her the opportunity and then encouraged her along the way. Today she can speak in front of 2,000 people and do a marvelous job. She's a perfect example of what it means to care for people and give them an opportunity."

George's service credo is not just limited to his relationships with his employees. As the operator of a disaster restoration business, he knows the trauma people go through when faced with unexpected tragedy. "On one occasion a prominent person in the community called me because his son had taken his own life, and he needed our help. When he called and talked to us about it, he could hardly get through the story. We said, 'Just leave it to us.' Later on that man called and said, 'I don't know how we would have gotten through this terrible situation if it hadn't been for ServiceMaster.' Whether it is an elderly person who wakes up in the morning and puts their feet into two inches of water or someone whose home has just burned, we have a great opportunity to help people. That's the thing that makes you love the business."

Although George has had to endure some great difficulties and personal disappointments, he's never let his circumstances defeat him. "If you don't have nerves of iron and an absolute tenacious desire to overcome problems, they can get the best of you. You have to have the mindset that 'this too will pass.' With God's help you will be able to overcome. He knows our needs and will provide. I believe that with my whole heart and soul. Trust in the Lord and don't despair. Life is hopeless without an anchor," George stated.

What can an unlearned child of a poor Dutch immigrant accomplish in his life? Ask the hundreds of people who love George and who have been changed for the better simply because they were blessed enough to know him. In one chorus they would all say, "George Meyer is a man who cares." And George, in his unassuming humble way, might smile and say, "What else could I have done to honor the God who has so honored me?"

THE TRUE REWARD: LIFELONG FRIENDSHIPS

The Story of John Emmons

"We were all one big family, working for God."
Marion E. Wade[1]

In the mid-1940s Marion E. Wade, the founder of ServiceMaster, had come to a realization. "I faced the fact," he wrote, "that if we were going to become a big organization, I would need the help of men who had a better head for business than I had. Now that the Lord had blessed me with the idea for the new rug-cleaning process, I didn't want to ruin it by my inexperience. Facing that need, I asked God to help me."[2] So on January 1, 1947, Marion Wade signed incorporation papers, and Wade, Wenger, and Associates was in business. Each of the men involved, Marion E. Wade, Bob Wenger, Ken Hansen, and others, had seen the great business potential in rug and carpet cleaning. Along with their business acumen, each had strong ethical foundation, and life-long relationships were formed that would eventually influence and nurture thousands of other businessmen.

In the early 1950s, just three short years after Wade, Wenger, and Associates had been formed, John Emmons graduated from Boston College Graduate School and was contemplating a career in the wool industry. It so happened that John's uncle owned the largest rug cleaning company in the world at that time, Albany Carpet Cleaning, located in Boston, Massachusetts. John joined his uncle's team as a sales manager.

Albany Carpet Cleaning performed a service that was needful then. In those days, people had area and oriental rugs that they sent into a plant to be cleaned during the summer. The company would clean the rugs and store them until they were to be delivered back to the owners in the fall.

In the 1950s Boston was a great center of the wool brokerage market, but the market was changing. Synthetic fibers were being developed, and wall-to-wall carpeting was becoming more and more affordable. The use of wool area rugs was about to become a luxury, and John and his uncle could see that change was fast approaching. With the advent of wall-to-wall carpeting, Albany was looking for a company that would provide the systems for them to handle the in-home carpet cleaning jobs. Albany Carpet Cleaning made an agreement with a new cutting-edge business out of Chicago, ServiceMaster.

John has fond memories of his meetings with the representatives of this young, growing company. "Marion recruited me into the business," he recalled. "The company was aggressive and sales-oriented. They seemed to be working on the front end, rather than the back edge, of a trend. Marion was a charismatic guy," John fondly remembered. "We loved him, and so our relationship worked out fine."

The business relationship between Albany Carpet Cleaning and ServiceMaster progressed, and eventually the time came when the contracts between the companies needed to be renewed. John's uncle was tardy in making the decision to stay with ServiceMaster, and in the meantime, Ken Hansen offered John several options to join with ServiceMaster. Once John's uncle finally decided to go with ServiceMaster, Hansen stuck by John and kept his promise to him, even though it made negotiations difficult with his uncle. "Mr. Hansen kept his word," John remembered. "That took a lot of gumption. He stood with me at that time when it would have been easy for him not to. He had integrity."

NO BUSINESS

In 1958, John bought a direct service license from ServiceMaster. He remembers the struggle of those early days: "I bought an opportunity that was just emerging. There wasn't a large staff offering support at that time. They just shipped some equipment to me, and Warren Wigand, a regional fellow, came in to help me unpack the stuff. He actually cried when he had to leave the next day because he wanted to stay with me and help me get started. So I had to get out and visit several people who had successful carpet retail businesses in the area. They helped me get started. Of course, my wife Marjorie really helped me and did a wonderful job." As a testimony to their faithful labor, John and Marjorie, along with their partners Bob and Joanne Fallon, received the Marion E. Wade Master Award in 1983.

Reflecting back on his decision to join with Service-Master, John wonders at his nerve. "I don't know how I had the courage to leave the family business and start out on my own. I am aggressive, honest, and hardworking, but not too smart. Still, I knew I could make it working for myself and liked the idea of being my own boss. I said to myself, *I am going to do it for somebody, why not me?* I really like people, and I'm fortunate that people like me, too."

"We all loved Marion so much," John stated. "So, in the early 1970s at the twenty-fifth anniversary of the company, we wanted to do something for him. I spearheaded a drive for the Master Franchisor Association (MFA) and collected around $6,000. That was a lot of money for that time. We bought him the finest golf cart that money could buy. I had the pleasure of driving that cart down the center aisle at the shareholders' meeting and presenting it to him."

FRIENDS SHARING A DREAM

As John looks over his 50 years with the company, he says that the greatest blessing he has received has come to him in the form of friends, some of them a surprise to him.

"At first, Ken Wessner seemed like a 'cold fish' to me," John admitted. "But as time went on, and we played a lot of golf together, he and I became great friends. In his last days when he was dying, I called just to ask his wife, Norma, how he was doing. She said, 'He would love to talk to you.' We talked for an hour and a half. I was so impressed by this that I called him back a week later, and it was the same story. He just wanted to have a buddy." John was a friend to Ken Wessner, and he's had numbers of other buddies throughout the years.

"I've made so many friends with guys from the ServiceMaster family, like Gerry Farrelly, Bill Emberlin, George Meyer, Thane MacNeill, Cal Flaig, Chuck Hodgin, and Bill Sunderland. I have friends all over the world," John boasted. "My brother used to tell me that I was the luckiest man in the world. I would say, 'I know I'm lucky, but you tell me why.' He would say, 'Look at all the pals you have got. You can go to any city in North America, and you have five great pals all the same age. You have all gone through the same thing, you love each other, and you have fun!' We were all young guys in our late twenties and early thirties, and nobody had any money. We had all these wonderful people—all aggressive, bright go-getters in the business—and we had more fun. We had all caught the same dream, thanks to Marion Wade."

The comradery these men enjoyed was fostered first by the fact that they had to help each other. "If I named my 12 closest friends, six or seven of them would be ServiceMaster people. The relationships that I had in ServiceMaster made such an impression on my brother that he finally started his own business."

John was also instrumental in helping others to catch the dream. He tells the story of Bob, a friend of his, who at one time had some extra discretionary money and offered it to John, interest-free. Since John was just starting out in the business and needed the help, he took his friend's offer, but repaid the loan over three years at 10 percent interest. As it turned out, Bob eventually sold his family business and was looking for a new opportunity. Bob and John started a commercial services business together. Then Bob developed a wonderful distributorship business. He eventually sold his distributorship and has retired and, according to John, "lives happily in Cape Cod."

THE IDEA REVIEW COUNCIL

As part of the original franchise group, John was instrumental in forming the Idea Review Council in the late 1970s. This council evolved to include distributors and then allowed franchisees to participate, Mike Isakson being the first. Now named the Franchise Council, it consists exclusively of franchise owners and acts as a liaison between the franchisee and the ServiceMaster home office.

John Emmons was also involved in the establishment of the Master Franchisor Association, or the MFA. This association was instrumental in accomplishing many things for the ServiceMaster family, including the origination and funding of the Marion E. Wade Scholarship fund. They also helped develop the potential in the disaster restoration business. Tom Gandee, a MFA member, developed the Quality Restoration Vendor program and Thane MacNeill, also a member, conceived the spot light commercial carpet cleaning concept.

These accomplishments, and many others, were made possible because of the warmhearted relationships that had been formed by the early pioneers in the service business.

NURTURING OTHERS

John's business philosophy is simple: If he's nurturing someone, he's happy. "I have been able to help people develop and convince several people to go into business. In fact," John said, "I have the happy reflection of knowing that I helped to make five or six multimillionaires."

Skip Fryling is a classic example of a success nurtured by John Emmons. "His wife had just had twins and he was a salesman and an honest guy. Now he has a very successful business. He has achieved all the things he wanted to achieve by his own efforts and by paying attention to what various distributors would suggest to him about continuing to run on the tracks laid out before them."

Although John has been successful financially, he doesn't measure success by mere monetary wealth. "Success is being respected by everyone you deal with. It is not a money thing. I don't have a lot of money, but I have a great time and have many marvelous friends."

John is also highly respected in the disaster restoration business because he's kept to the high standards he saw in the founders of ServiceMaster. "I don't promise more than I can deliver, and I always deliver more than I promise," he stated emphatically. "I've never left a customer without doing something additional for them simply because I like them, and I want their ongoing business."

In the years since he first joined with Wade, Wenger, and Associates, John has seen great transformations in the business. From in-plant wool rug cleaning to on-location housewide disaster restoration, he's had to remain flexible and be willing to change. "Change everything," that is, "except the basic foundation." Part of that foundation is standing behind what he does, and John admits that over the years this has cost him a lot of money. To John, there are certain non-negotiables in his business, and ethical standards are one of them. "I'm big on integrity. There is not a single person I've knowingly mistreated in my life."

Every one of John's five children have been involved in the ServiceMaster family over the years. His daughter Judy runs an excellent ServiceMaster organization north of Boston. Each child has had the opportunity to get to know the people in the company and to love them.

The ServiceMaster family means different things to different people. To some it means financial independence, to others it is the opportunity to chart your own course. To still others it means having the opportunity to produce a quality product, establish a reputation, and build your dreams. John Emmons has accomplished all this, but ServiceMaster means something more to him: it means lifelong friendships forged through years of trailblazing, difficulty, and growth. It means that he can look back over his life's work and name the names of people he has nurtured and who have nurtured him. It means that he's got pals across the country, and it has been these affectionate relationships that have made his 50-year stay with the ServiceMaster Clean family both profitable, and in the end, a really fun journey.

"WE ARE FAMILY"

The Story of the George and Lula Holland Family

*"Playing as a dedicated team member was the
only way to become important to them."*
Marion E. Wade[1]

In 1954 George and Lula Holland were the owners of
New Beauty Rug Cleaners in Hutchison, Kansas. With
the development of wall-to-wall carpeting, George decided
to try his hand at on-location cleaning.

"My father had actually tried to clean four or five
homes with wall-to-wall carpeting," his son John said. "He
thought he could clean carpets the same way that he cleaned
loose rugs in the plant. He used a garden hose and a bucket
of banana oil shampoo that he just threw on the carpet. He
not only ruined the carpets but also ruined the oak floors
underneath. He then decided that he would never do another

on-location carpet cleaning. That was until he met Harry Heard, a salesman for ServiceMaster."

"I'm in the business of putting people into the carpet-cleaning business," Harry informed him.

"Well, I'm already in the carpet-cleaning business," was George's terse reply.

"No, you're in the rug-cleaning business. If you join with ServiceMaster, we'll teach you how to clean wall-to-wall carpeting."

THOSE CLEVER GUYS

On May 1, 1954, George and "Lu" Holland purchased the forty-second on-location ServiceMaster franchise. "They paid $500—hard-earned money—for which they received a roto, a tank vacuum, a wall-cleaning machine, a few chemicals, and a four-percent fee structure," John remembers. "I joined them in the business almost immediately, but when I turned 12, I actually began to work."

George's first real introduction to the ServiceMaster comradery and family came during his training in Chicago. Ken Hansen was teaching marketing and took George to do "blockbusting" in a certain neighborhood. They knocked on doors, trying to sell carpet cleaning jobs. At one particular door, after Ken had gotten about halfway through the presentation, he turned to George and said, "Okay, George, now you take over. Finish the sale." Although George felt terribly awkward, he turned the cold call into a sale, and his career with ServiceMaster was off and running.

When George returned home after his training, John remembers his dad's report to the family. "Those clever guys just sold me my business again."

George's business grew steadily, and in 1958 the family could afford to purchase a new home. John, whose main job was as a "roto jockey," remembers that as time went on, his father wanted him to become involved in other aspects of the business. "So, in 1965, he sent me to the Academy of Service, where I met Dale Stephson, my instructor. My father wanted me to learn sales and management, but I really didn't want to be at the academy, which became obvious to everyone very quickly."

"Dale, my instructor, took me aside and said, 'John, your attitude is hurting our other new franchisees. Straighten up, or I will send you home.' Soon afterward, he came back to me and said, 'You're wasting your father's money.' He took me to the train station for the ten-hour ride back home. The closer I got to home, the louder the click-clack of the train wheels on the tracks became. I will never forget how loud that noise was. When I got off the train, my father said to me, 'Son, I am very disappointed in you. You have embarrassed your mother and I with the ServiceMaster company. Get in the car.'" Needless to say, John began to look at the business in a different way from that time on.

"In 1964, my father sent my wife, Janet, and I to the Mayo Hotel in Tulsa, Oklahoma to attend our very first seminar. My dad wanted us to meet as many of the franchisees as we could so that we would be challenged and learn from them. I was only 22," John recalls. "Ken Hansen was presenting a seminar on budgeting and controlling finances. We didn't have a lot of money at the time, so my father asked us to try to conserve as much as we could. At the conclusion of the first day many of the attendees were standing in the foyer of the hotel, deciding which fancy restaurant to go to. Because Janet and I knew that we couldn't afford to go with them, we were trying to slip out surreptitiously. It was then that Marion E. Wade turned and saw us."

"'Where are you going to dinner?' he asked. I was embarrassed, and while I was trying to think of something to say, he realized our problem. He put his arms around us and said, 'How about joining us as our guests?' We didn't know how to refuse him, so off we went to a fancy French restaurant. When the waiter came to Janet and me, it was obvious to Marion E. Wade that we didn't know how to read the menu, so he said, 'Why don't you let me order for you?' What a relief!"

"Marion E. Wade embodied the ServiceMaster ethic of caring for others. Our interaction with him was a very powerful influence in our lives. He gave us a family perspective," John said. "I learned that ServiceMaster was a family, and he had made us feel like we were part of that family. That's a valuable lesson that's impacted the way that we've treated others through the years. He knew that we felt awkward and couldn't carry on a conversation with the others at our table, so he sat close to us. I've never forgotten that I need to reach out to people I don't know. Although Marion E. Wade knew many, many people, he never forgot who we were. I recall several subsequent occasions when he stopped to speak with us personally. That was just the way he was."

BETTING THE EGG MONEY

In 1968, after attending a national convention in Chicago, George "bet the egg money again" and purchased a distributorship for western Kansas. "Dad had to buy 10 franchises for a thousand dollars a piece," John said. "That meant that he had to come up with $10,000. In those days that was a lot of money. But the company helped work out a financial program for him. When we were getting off the train after returning from Chicago, dad said, 'Those clever guys just sold me my territory again!'"

George began to focus on selling franchises in his area. First he analyzed his territory and decided where he thought the franchises should be. Then he and his son John would load up the car with First Aid Spotting Kits. As they drove through Kansas, they would talk to insurance agents and adjusters, as well as managers of carpet and furniture stores, about providing ServiceMaster cleaning through their facilities. While journeying from town to town they were looking for possible franchisees and passing out the Spotting Kits. They eventually set up a considerable network in these small towns, which helped them to begin to sell franchises.

Because George believed in the four corporate objectives, he actively sought ways to help people develop. He recognized that there were a lot of people who wanted to get into the business but didn't have the money. So he developed a program to help them. "We would set up a business and get it up and running with our investment, and then we would find a buyer for it in a year or two. Although these people didn't have cash, they were able to give us sweat-equity for the business. We would move the new buyer in, and then we would proceed on to another town," John said. "My wife Jan and I had the responsibility of developing those businesses. The first time we went on our own, my dad told us that we needed to go to Great Bend, Kansas and set up a franchise there. That was his way of developing people." Not only was it his way of developing strangers and adopting them into the ServiceMaster family, it was the way that George had discovered to develop his own son, John.

"I told my dad I didn't want to do it," John confesses. "I didn't think I could do the sales. He said, 'You're going to go do it.' So in 1968 he gave us $500 and a set of equipment. Then he told me that he was coming over to Great Bend, and we were going to go out and do 'blockbusting.' He was going to teach me how to sell."

George arrived at John's house on a Sunday in the middle of January in 1968. It snowed all during the night, and on Monday morning the ground was covered with more than ten inches of snow. "I thought, *Good, now we can't go*," John admits. "But my dad said, 'We're going.' We had to put on those ServiceMaster white smocks and go traipsing through the snow without any boots or coats. We were freezing to death. We were actually very successful that day because many of the women felt sorry for us and invited us in to have coffee and warm up. That neighborhood in Great Bend where we did those initial calls has remained one of our most successful areas for years. 'Now you're off and running,' my dad said. 'See you next week.'"

Four Bags of Groceries

John remembers that his early work ethic was not very admirable. "I was always late to work. My dad hired me only one more time than he fired me. So, when we went to Great Bend, and I was my own boss, I decided that I was going to do paperwork at 8:00 in the morning and schedule the first job at 8:30. It wasn't long before I was sleeping in late. Then I would go to lunch about 11:45, make a couple of phone calls, schedule a job about 1:30 or 2:00, and then be finished by 4:00 p.m. I figured that I couldn't work later than that because I wanted to be at home when the children were finished with school. I don't know where I got the impression that this mindset would work. Soon it became apparent that we were running out of money. I really started to change when Janet came to me and said, 'There is only $20 left. I can't buy our four bags of groceries this week; I can only buy two. I highly recommend that you be out of the house tomorrow morning before 8:00 a.m.' That was the kicker that I needed. I wasn't going to let my kids go hungry."

John and Janet built the business in Great Bend and sold it off after about a year. Then they went to Hutchison and ran the operation for a year while George went north to set up a business in Salina, Kansas. Along with John's brother-in-law, Dave Cowles, they set up and sold off nearly ten businesses. "We had great market penetration. What we did worked."

The Hollands looked at each of their franchisees as family, and they were helped greatly by others, including Gene Nichol and Jesse Berthume. The family aspect of ServiceMaster was so extraordinarily important to John's father George simply because he didn't have one when he was young.

You're Too Old to Stay Here

In 1922, when George was only 11, a flu epidemic swept through his town. His mother succumbed to the epidemic, as did his sister. His father, who was a railroader for the Santa

Fe, put George and his two siblings in an orphanage in Pueblo, Colorado. Because these were troubled times in the country, the orphanage was overloaded. Three years later the director of the orphanage came to George and said, "We have too many kids here, so everyone who is 14 years of age and above has to leave." George contacted his father who suggested that he try to get to Kansas to see if he could live with his aunt there. Young George made his way to Hutchison, Kansas and just showed up on the doorstep of his aunt. It was there in Hutchison that George finally found a home and made one for so many others.

"Family was important to my dad," said John. "When he sold a franchise, it wasn't just a business deal; he was selling to a friend. He made every franchisee part of his family. We still have a number of franchisees who have been in business 20-25 years."

In 1976, George suddenly passed away from a heart attack. "It's still hard for me to talk about it," John said tearfully. "Bob De Jong, another part of our ServiceMaster family, stepped in and helped me during that time. He taught me that it was now my responsibility to take my dad's place in the distributorship. 'You've got to learn how to teach your franchisees to run their businesses,' Bob told me. It was Bob who forced me to put on a workshop for the franchisees and ultimately gave me the confidence that I needed. Bob became a confidant, a second father to me. He gave me incredible support, and so did Bob Groff later on."

In 1981 John and his brother-in-law, Dave Cowles, won the Marion E. Wade award. "That was an emotional time for us because we knew that was really just a recognition of the work that mom and dad had done. They would have loved to receive it."

MADE TO MEASURE

John and Janet still have a golden ruler that was given to them at a conference in 1964. The ruler is inscribed with the phrase "Made to Measure." "We've kept that ruler because it reminds us of Marion and his commitment to family. He often said his dream was to travel across the United States and stop at ServiceMaster franchises in every town so he could visit members of his 'extended family.'"

"My father came to Dave and I one day in 1972 and said, 'Sons, give me your youth, and I will give you my knowledge and wisdom, and we will build a very successful business in Kansas.'" From their humble beginnings to a highly successful distributor business, George's love of family and commitment to others has kept the family together.

BLEEDING YELLOW

In 1995 John and Dave sold their distributorships and went to work for the home office. Although they don't have the day-to-day relationship with the franchisees that they love, they know that they are helping further the vision of ServiceMaster Clean—a vision of family, heritage, and caring.

"We want all of our associates to understand the ServiceMaster culture. We can't teach people to care, but we can help them focus on caring if it's already in their heart. We want each person to feel so much a part of this great family that if you were to cut them they would bleed yellow." For the past three decades, John has been one who has bled yellow in all that he says and does in his relationships with others—a trait that he surely inherited from his mother and father, and a trait has been transfused into others by his example.

TRAINING AND TRAILBLAZING

The Story of Gerry Farrelly and Phil Fitzpatrick

"The pursuit of excellence is what broadens a man and his horizon."

Marion E. Wade[1]

In light of the fact that Gerry Farrelly and his eight siblings grew up in the Chicago area, it was probably inevitable that he would end up in ServiceMaster, although he would have told you he really wasn't interested in owning his own business.

His father owned a small department store selling clothing and housewares, a sort of mini-Sears. Gerry recalled his childhood opinion of business ownership. "Seeing how my father worked basically seven days a week, I never had any intention of being an entrepreneur. I worked in the store every single day after school, and on Saturdays when I was in high school. I would have worked on Sundays, but thank God," Gerry laughed, "in those days stores weren't open on Sundays. We even worked three nights a week until after 9:00 p.m. We had late dinners at our house, as you can imagine. I vowed I would never go into business for myself. I hated retail work. I was going to be a chemical engineer."

So, in April of 1959, after graduating from college, Gerry took a position with Wade, Wenger and Associates as a chemical engineer. He worked in the laboratory directly for Bernie Cozett, an early pioneer in the business. Soon after, when the company moved to Downer's Grove and changed its name to ServiceMaster, someone was needed to take over the plant operations. "I was the only guy around who knew how to mix one chemical with another," Gerry humbly stated, "so, they gave me the job." For three years Gerry developed the technical side of the janitorial business cleaning systems and manuals. In September 1962, the hospital division of the company was starting to burgeon, and Gerry's expertise was needed elsewhere. He went to work for Ken Wessner training and overseeing ServiceMaster's operations at Lutheran General Hospital. He would stay at one hospital until he had trained someone else to oversee it, then he would move on to another. This division was growing exponentially at the time, and eventually the decision was made for Gerry to become the general operations manager. He stayed in that position until August of 1969, when with Denis Horsfall, he decided to purchase a franchise in San Diego, California.

Although Gerry really loved his job in the hospital division, he recalls the travel as brutal. "I would be gone for two or three weeks and then come home on Friday and go back out on Sunday. Denis Horsfall was the top salesman in the division, and he was gone from his family all the time. Denis would come home on Saturday afternoon, go to church on Sunday morning, and then on Sunday afternoon he would hop back in the car and take off again. The travel was the major reason we left. I was gone on every single holiday, every Christmas." During one particularly grueling trip, when he and Denis were snowed-in the week between Christmas and New Years in Lincoln, Nebraska, they talked over the possibilities of owning their own business.

By 1969 the decision had been made, and Denis and Gerry went to San Diego and purchased an existing franchise. Denis was to be the salesman, and Gerry would run operations. But the business was struggling financially. Denis needed to earn more money than the business could provide, so in the early 1970s he decided that he had to leave and go back into sales. Growing the business was taking too long, and Gerry remembers Denis' leaving with much regret. "He was a great salesman," Gerry recalled. "I really missed him when he left. He was a good man."

Gerry knew that phenomenal growth was possible. He'd seen it happen in the hospital division, which had started with zero employees and had grown to 3,500 when he left. But he was having trouble getting insurance adjusters to give him a chance.

THE KITCHEN CREEK FIRE

Gerry had been knocking on insurance adjusters' doors for months and wasn't getting anywhere. Then in 1971, disaster struck San Diego County, and overnight everybody in the disaster restoration industry was overwhelmed.

During one of San Diego's infamous Santa Ana weather patterns, when hot desert winds race across the county toward the ocean, a small fire began in Pine Valley (a mountainous suburb on the east side of the county) and quickly spread west, consuming thousands of acres. The Kitchen Creek Fire, as it was named, was one of the largest fires in San Diego history, and insurance adjusters and agents were so overwhelmed with losses they began picking names out of the phone book.

Gerry recalled this as a key time for his young business. "Adjusters gave us a chance and saw that we did a good job and our prices weren't crazy. Because there was so much work, all the other companies were gouging the adjusters, but our prices were right. Once we handled all this work from the fire, we had proven that we could do a decent job, and they knew we weren't going to cheat them. This fire is what really started the business. We went from just breaking even to making a significant profit overnight."

Gerry decided that his business would concentrate almost solely on insurance work. "I wanted to be known as the best contents guy in San Diego." Gerry realized that the business would grow if he produced quality work. Although specializing solely in disaster restoration work was a novel approach, he was convinced that the insurance business was much more profitable than mere home cleaning. Gerry began looking for men that he could bring into the business and train.

In the early 1970s Phil Fitzpatrick was finishing his degree from a local Bible college. During school he had been the assistant manager of a restaurant, but in 1975 he had lost his job and was looking for a new career. A friend provided him with a carpet cleaning machine, and he started a small residential cleaning business. The business quickly failed, however, and Phil found himself and his little family terribly in debt. He contacted Sears to see if there was an opening in their home-cleaning department. At that time ServiceMaster was doing all of Sears' carpet cleaning, and he was told to contact Gerry Farrelly. He interviewed with ServiceMaster and accepted a position with them in 1976.

QUALITY AND INNOVATION

Phil remembers those difficult times. "My initial goal was just to pay my bills and feed my family. I made only $2.65 an hour, but it helped us get out of the hole." Phil started as a carpet cleaner and then learned to do carpet installation as well. "Gerry had this novel idea to develop a team that focused solely on flood work. In those days, all the workers did every kind of job, but Gerry saw that specialization within each division of the company would work out best. I think that Gerry was the first in ServiceMaster who had a crew that specialized in carpet installation and cleaning in one visit."

Gerry's business grew rapidly, and the news of his success was spreading in the ServiceMaster family. "In those days we had one of the largest disaster restoration businesses in the nation," Phil recalled. "People used to come from all over to visit our office and see how we were doing things. We opened our doors to everyone."

During these early years computers were just beginning to make their debut in small businesses, so Gerry developed a computer program that could do job estimations that other franchisees from around the nation used. Phil boasted, "Gerry was a pioneer in the disaster restoration business. He knew that specialization was key, and he developed the operating systems to support each division." Just as Gerry had developed the janitorial manuals during his tenure at ServiceMaster in Chicago, he organized new ways of doing things in his business.Gerry's business credo followed that of the founders, especially Ken Wessner, who was known as an extraordinarily hard worker. "Work hard and do a good job" were the keys to his business' success. "Produce quality work and charge reasonable prices."

Phil's managerial skills were soon noticed by Gerry, who brought him in from the field—first as a manager of the flood division, and then eventually as manager of the entire insurance division.

TIME FOR CHANGE

In 1987, after successfully building the business, Gerry decided to split the San Diego territory into north and south county businesses. Gerry sold the south business and then helped Phil to set up the business in the north.

"When I started I knew that there was a tremendous risk," Phil said. "I knew how quickly we could get into debt and be in a position of failure. We needed profit, so we didn't hire many employees. I did a lot of the work myself and was on call 24 hours a day. During the first five years, I didn't take a vacation because we needed to produce a bottom line that was profitable. Soon Gerry became a partner in the business and provided the financial stability we needed to continue to support the growth of the company."

Following in the footsteps of the founders, Phil still relies tenaciously on their beliefs. "What has helped me all along is a strong faith, my foundational belief in Jesus as my personal Savior," Phil confessed. "I think the security of knowing that nothing would happen to me beyond His control has given me confidence through the years. So, no matter how intimidating the situation may appear, I know that God is here and in control, even though I might not see an immediate answer."

"I DON'T WANT YOU TO TAKE A LOSS"

Gerry remembers the character of Marion Wade and Ken Hansen. While he was still working in the hospital division, Marion Wade mentioned to Gerry that he was going to donate ServiceMaster stock to Wheaton College.

"You young people should have stock in the company," Marion said to Gerry.

"I would like to," Gerry replied, "but I don't have that kind of money."

"Come with me," Marion said. He took Gerry into the controller's office and said, "Gerry wants to buy stock, and I want the company to loan him $2,000. Don't charge him any interest. He can pay the loan back at $50 a month."

A few weeks later, however, the stock fell from $20 a share to $17. Marion searched Gerry out and said, "I don't want you to take a loss on that stock."

"Don't worry, it will come back," Gerry replied.

But Marion worked it out so that Gerry got the stock for $17 instead of $20.

"He didn't have to do that," Gerry testified. "But he did it because it was the honorable thing."

Phil remembers Ken Hansen as an honorable man, too. "Ken was accessible and had real loyalty to the franchisees and to ServiceMaster. I remember the last time I saw Ken. We were having a meeting in Santa Barbara, where he had retired. He had had one eye removed and was weak, but he stopped by our meeting. He came in just long enough to tell us to continue the good work and say, "God bless you." Then he left. He still felt the connection with the franchisees. That kind of dedication has made a direct impression on me," Phil said with admiration.

THE TRADITION CONTINUES

Phil's desire is that the founders' beliefs continue to permeate the company. "We took four months last year to go over the corporate objectives in our employee meetings. I want the employees to recognize how they play out in our business. It is good to see them posted on the wall," Phil said, "but I want the employees to see what they mean. Everybody has a perception of what God would expect of them, whether they believe in Him or not. People know about fundamental moral standards. I want them to grasp these standards, and I'm happy that they're operating in our business."

As Gerry has observed the quality of the work produced in the north county office, he can see that his credo is continuing. "The Escondido office has a better product than I or anybody I have ever seen delivers. Everyone that has ever come through the Escondido business comments that the quality of the work product is just exceptional." Phil echoes this thought: "There is a persona our company has. We want to be on the cutting edge; we want to be leaders in the industry."

SOWING AND REAPING

Gerry and Phil were joined in partnership in the early 1990s by Michael Gamez. In addition to his duties as an owner, Michael oversees the fire division and has a fantastic reputation in the insurance industry. Today ServiceMaster Complete Restoration in Escondido, California, employs 75 and has received the President's Cabinet award given to the five top On Location revenue producers. They've added a disaster restoration office in Orange County and have also begun commercial services operations. Although they've grown exponentially, their fundamental focus on producing a quality product and conducting business honestly has never wavered.

"We still want to be known as the best in the business, but that's not all. We also want our employees to know that we're interested in their development. For instance, we've extended health insurance to employees who have left us just so that they would have medical care while they looked for other job opportunities. We've taken the whole company and their families to Disneyland. We give away thousands of dollars annually in performance and Christmas bonuses. We want our employees to know that we're more concerned about their well-being than our profitability."

"People like Gerry Farrelly have helped me tremendously," Phil acknowledged. "So, I think it is part of my responsibility to do that for others. If I have the ability or opportunity to help someone else—an employee or even other ServiceMaster franchises—I do, even if it doesn't directly affect me."

Today Phil spends about 15-20 percent of his time training other franchisees, and even adjusters who are out of his area. "I believe it is a principle of sowing and reaping. I am more interested in pleasing God and thinking about how He sees me than anything else. I strive to please God, and I think that means helping others, even if that doesn't result in an immediate benefit for our business. That isn't important. In the end, God will make all that happen."

In his ongoing efforts to help others develop, Phil was instrumental in establishing the Admiral's Club, an association of the top 25 disaster restoration and top five Construction businesses in the ServiceMaster Clean family. They meet at the QRV (Quality Restoration Vendor) and national conventions, sharing their expertise with each other. In 1999, Phil and Mike received the Ken Hansen Award. This award is given to a franchisee for outstanding philanthropic work in the community. This award is a demonstration of the heart of the owners of ServiceMaster Complete Restoration. "We want to sow into others' lives. We're committed to that."

ServiceMaster has provided career opportunities for both Phil and Mike's families. Phil's son, James, has worked in the marketing department; his son-in-law, Cody, oversees the water division; while his son, Joel, manages the newly acquired commercial services operation. Mike's brother Raphael, brother-in-law Larry and Larry's wife Annie work in the fire division. His mother, Juanita, oversees the laundry services, and his stepfather, Rapha, works in their 20,000-square-foot plant. In addition, many of their employees have family members who work in the business. "That says a lot to us," Phil commented. "When an employee wants his family to work in the business, that means we're taking care of them."

"We have a high moral standard coupled with a high work standard. We operate by these standards, and our customers know that they can trust us. We are honest. We have the same reputation that Gerry established years ago. We're still giving them the best possible product for the best price. We are trying to look out for their interest. But it isn't always easy. At every loss site we're confronted with the opportunity to change our ethics. Mike and I are endeavoring to hold the line against compromising the quality of service that founders like Wade, Hansen, and Wessner established. Gerry wanted to be known for the quality of the product in his business, and we're still trying to do that."

When Gerry Farrelly took an entry-level position mixing chemicals for a fledgling young company, he had no idea where it would lead him. His journey has given him the opportunity to observe the quality of character and concern at the very foundations of the ServiceMaster Clean business and then to pass that on to others. It is only right that Phil and Mike seek to produce the highest quality and help others achieve it as well. They're following the path that's been set out before them.

INTEGRITY AND INDIVIDUAL ACHIEVEMENT:
Fulfilling the American Dream

The Story of George Jr. and David Albino

"I wanted a job where my income would depend on my individual performance."
Marion E. Wade[1]

As young Nicolas Albino looked out over the city of Benevento in Southern Italy, he came to a monumental decision. Even though Southern Italy had been reunified with the rest of the country, the people of Benevento weren't experiencing much prosperity. This city, which had once been fought over by the Goths and the Byzantines, was part of the depressed economy of Campania, where aside from agriculture and the industries that it spawned, there wasn't much work and even less hope of economic freedom or growth. But Nicolas had one skill: working with leather products, particularly shoes. So he saved his money, and, like many other Italians in the early twentieth century, bought passage on a steamer for America, the land of opportunity. He hoped that it was there he would be able to turn his skill and willingness to work hard into a life of freedom and success.

As a young, single man, Nicolas had a vision of prosperity not only for himself but for his descendants. The seeds of the great American entrepreneurial ideal of working hard and carving out a legacy were blooming in his young heart. So, in 1923, after saving his meager earnings from working at a shoe factory in Boston, he opened his own shoe repair store in Waterbury, Connecticut. It was in this shop that his sons George, Sr. and Jerome would work for years to come, pursuing their dream, treating their customers with respect and operating with integrity.

Eventually his son George, Sr. opened his own shop in a modest 60 x 40 building, where he, in turn, would teach his sons (George, Jr. and Allan) the shoemaking and shoe repairing skills that would provide their livelihood for years to come. Today George Jr.'s brother Allan continues a tradition of the Waterbury, Connecticut enterprise that has spanned more than 78 years.

The story of Nicolas' grandson, George, Jr., his wife Elaine, their son David, and his wife Kathleen, is an American story that's been retold millions of times. With little education and no family advantage, the aspirations of one man with the courage and the vision to take a risk was fulfilled. Today, George, Jr. and his son David operate a thriving disaster restoration business in Waterbury. It's a business that has not only supported them financially, but has also given them the opportunity to work together, build a strong family and serve others. It's given them the freedom to set their own standards, develop their own skills and build genuine and lasting relationships with their employees and customers. But most of all, it's been the venue where George, Jr. has been given the opportunity to be the arbiter of his own success. He would succeed or fail based on his own hard work, ingenuity, enthusiasm, and perseverance.

TURNING SHOE LEATHER INTO GOLD

In 1959 George, Jr's. workday was spent, as it had been since his childhood, in his shoe repair store. Although he worked industriously, the prospects of great success or wealth were dim. The most he could expect to earn from any sale was less than five dollars, and although he was thankful for the steady work, he knew that he and his wife Elaine could achieve so much more if they just had the chance.

In August of 1959 Elaine's father, Frank Lacilla, was intrigued by and pursued information about a new company called ServiceMaster. He had read their story in *Reader's Digest* and found the concept of owning a carpet cleaning business interesting. Art Melvin, ServiceMaster's representative, met with the family, and they decided to purchase a franchise. Since Frank didn't have the capital needed to start the business, George arranged the financing, using the shoe shop as collateral. And so it was that Grandfather Nicholas' desire for freedom and opportunity opened the door for his grandson's family to experience the kind of independence that he had only dreamt of. In December of 1959, the business was begun. Although the family was excited about the prospects of operating their own business, they didn't know then that they had embarked on what would become a fantastic journey that would alter the course and character of their lives and would grow into something more splendid than they could possibly imagine.

From 1959 to October 1972, George continued to labor in the shoe repair shop with his brother, Allan. During the hours that the shop was open, George diligently served his clientele. Then, in the evenings and on weekends, he labored with the family in the ServiceMaster business. The days in the shoe shop were long and arduous, and he would routinely work for 14 hours in the shoe business and then spend the evening cleaning carpets.

George suspects that many people just don't understand the amount of work it takes to put a successful business together. "They don't know about the 12- to 14-hour days that you'll have to work. Long days," George smiles. "Thankfully, my wife is used to them." But the thought of going to work early in the morning and then not returning home until late in the evening wasn't unfamiliar to George. It was a lifestyle that had been modeled by his father and grandfather before him. It is the lifestyle that he has modeled for his son David, who is set to take over the business when his father retires. It is the lifestyle of not being afraid of honest work. During the early years of the business, George's home was the base of operation. The business' telephone rang in the kitchen of the Lacilla home, and the rugs were cleaned in the basement of George's house. But George's residence wasn't just a business; it was also a home for his children. On some days, after George, Frank, and Elizabeth (Frank's wife) had cleaned the carpets, he would discover that his children had playfully ridden their bikes over them, and the work would begin again.

Opportunities Open

Frank worked hard and diligently built the business over the years, and by 1969 it was very successful. He realized then that it was time to make some major growth moves.

So, in July 1969, Frank's son Dennis became a junior partner with his father and started the Contract Services division of the company. Frank continued to manage the growing on-location and disaster restoration portion of the business. But both of the divisions continued to grow, and by 1972 it became apparent that it was time for George to enter the business on a full-time basis, as a minority partner, heading up the disaster restoration side.

In his thirty-eighth year, the opportunity that George had visualized during the long days in the shoe repair shop had finally materialized. It was time to take risks, to give up the guaranteed security of the shoe shop, and face the greatest challenge of his life. It was time for George to cross his ocean.

From 1972 through 1986, George worked hard learning his new craft, including all of the skills required to build his division into a powerful and profitable business. By June of 1986 Dennis Lacilla had accomplished the same success in his contract services division and had become a distributor in contract services for Connecticut, New York, and Massachusetts. Frank had retired, and George and Dennis decided it was time to split the business. Dennis would keep the contract services business and George would take the on location/disaster restoration side, making it a stand-alone business.

George was finally in control of his own destiny, and all the decisions—right or wrong— would be made by him. George believed that disaster restoration would be the wave of the future and decided it was there that he would focus his efforts. At fifty-two years of age, he would be the captain of his fate and of his professional and financial future without the constraints or restrictions of having to defer to others. He was now free to chart his own course.

George's first major decision was to bring his son, David, into the business with him, and it's been a decision that he's never regretted. David's history in the family business and his enthusiasm, strength and determination have caused this father-son enterprise to flourish.

George wasn't afraid of hard work, and he knew that if he treated his customers with respect and empathy, he'd be successful. "Always give people more than they pay for," is more than a trite business saying to hang on a wall: it's the credo of ServiceMaster by Albino. Today, George and his son David operate a thriving disaster restoration business…but they haven't wandered far from the attitudes that Nicolas brought with him nearly a century ago from Italy.

CHARACTER CREATES EXCELLENCE

"I remember the days in the shoe repair shop when the most I could make on a sale, even when I did my best, was $3.95. It was there, in that place, that I learned from my father and grandfather that *the customer is always right*, no matter how insignificant the task." Although the compensation levels have increased greatly since those days, the principle of quality customer service continues to guide George's business practice today. If a customer isn't completely satisfied with the service, "We tell our technician to go back and do it again," George stated. "Even though he may tell us it is perfect, we still send him back. We know that we might be taken advantage of or abused, but I would rather be abused than have a reputation of not being trustworthy."

Integrity is the word that best describes the principles that guide George's business. It's the quality of honorable character that plays itself out primarily in his relationships with his customers. And it's the way that he exemplifies ServiceMaster's four corporate objectives. To George, honoring God simply means honoring and respecting his customers. "I always try to do something extra for my customers," he acknowledged, "and no one has ever been unhappy with that."

The confidence that comes from knowing that you've done more than the mere necessary requirements permeates George's relationships with his customers. "If you don't do a job well, you can't look your customer in the eye. Whether it's an insurance adjuster or a customer walking along the street, I'm confident that I can go up to him and shake his hand and ask him how he's doing. I've never had to duck and run somewhere." George enjoys the clean conscience that comes from following his father and grandfather's advice. Since childhood he's known the importance of understanding the wants and needs of his clients. "Something I knew since I was seven or eight years old was, 'Customer, customer,

customer...thank you ma'am, and thank you sir." It's a lesson that's never been eclipsed by his growth and success.

QUALITY CUSTOMER SERVICE STARTS WITH QUALITY EMPLOYEES

The employees at ServiceMaster of Waterbury learn what's expected of them because George and his son David set the standard by their example. Even today, when George might be letting up in his involvement, his employees have frequently seen him take off his tie and suit coat, roll up his sleeves, and show them how he wants the work accomplished. George and son David believe that they must lead their employees by example, just the way their forefathers did. "Our employees need to know that we're not afraid to work and that we don't think we're too good to get dirty with them."

George knows that when a technician enters a customer's home, he's there representing him. In fact, he believes that it's as though he walked in the room himself. He knows that the key to achieving the kind of quality service that he strives for is quality employees. "You could hit the road with the best equipment and the best chemicals, but that's all insignificant in comparison with how the customer is being served. That's the biggest challenge. Everything else is secondary."

George believes that employee retention is a major factor in high-quality production. The proof that he really prizes employee retention is demonstrated in the fact that the average stay for employees at his business is 19 years! To what does he attribute this longevity? "We treat our employees with dignity."

One facet of treating their employees with respect is delegation. The Albinos are firm believers in "giving employees the ball and letting them run with it." They believe that it's in this way that entry-level employees develop into leaders. "It's not that we aren't involved, though. We have our finger on the pulse of the business, and we watch the financial reports closely, but we also give our employees the freedom to do their jobs."

HONORS FROM THEIR PEERS

In 1997 the Albino's business was reviewed by Bob Knapp, a consultant who is employed by ServiceMaster Clean as a business financial and personal estate planning analyst. In a letter that George and Elaine cherish, Knapp wrote, "In all the years that I have been with ServiceMaster, I believe your business demonstrates as well as any I have seen the incredible potential of the ServiceMaster business opportunity. You have built an estate by careful control of your business and personal life...and your business would be a wonderful case study to challenge others to do likewise."

In reflecting on Knapp's letter, George said that he recognized that even though they aren't the biggest business in the country, "we are one of the best." Knowing that he has achieved this level of excellence is very significant to George, and it is a testimony to the opportunity for success that a ServiceMaster franchise offers.

THE TRUE MEANING OF SUCCESS: FAMILY VIRTUE

With the heritage that he's had, it's no wonder that George Albino thinks about success in terms of his family. For him, success isn't measured solely by his financial independence, but rather, by the bond of commitment and caliber of integrity in his household.

"Although I am proud of this business, it is not my legacy," he states unashamedly. "I am proud of this business, but to me my success is my family and the achievements of all of my children. One part of that success is that my son David will take over the business when I'm gone."

For George, success means that the ideals that were passed on to him from his father and grandfather have been passed on to his children. His greatest satisfaction comes from knowing that his children have been taught to be independent and to work hard. The business has merely been a vehicle to make a living; it has been the environment in which he could continue the tradition of influencing his children's character—a tradition that his predecessors began.

The humility and merit of character is seen in David Albino's perspective on his position as employer and soon-to-be owner. He's never too busy to listen to an employee, nor does he think that it is beneath him to accompany his workers on a difficult job, especially if it's a particularly dirty one. He has embraced the legacy of his forefathers: "No matter how successful you are, don't ever forget where you came from. Don't ever forget what you are doing. Basically you strip it all away, and we are cleaners. Don't ever lose sight of that." Diligently serving his customers in humility and honesty are qualities that David has made his own and that bode well for the future of the company as it continues onward in the twenty-first century.

George says, "As I look back over my work life I can do so with a great feeling of accomplishment and pride, both in the work that I did in the shoe shop and in our own business. There is dignity in working with your hands, whether that's in the context of shoe repair or cleaning the soot off of a suede couch." Indeed, George and David are both dignified men who have tasted for themselves the golden harvest of the American dream.

STANDING ON THE SHOULDERS
OF THEIR FATHERS

George, his wife Elaine, and David and Kathleen know that they're experiencing prosperity today because of the sweat, diligence, and honesty of their ancestors. Elaine's mother and father began their business late in life and worked long, hard hours to put the company on solid footing. From their humble beginnings throwing rugs in the back of an old

Chevy and taking them to George's basement for cleaning to the successful business they operate today, the Albinos are the quintessential portrait of the American dream.

Some people might say that the American dream is dead, but the Albinos would disagree. Nicolas believed that it was available to him, even though we can imagine that as he looked out over the ship's railing during his trip from Italy, he might have done so with some trepidation. He surely recognized that he wasn't bringing many advantages with him. He didn't have great wealth, a first-rate education, or a distinguished family history. But he did have one thing: He knew the dignity that came from hard work, honesty, and integrity. Coupled with the character modeled by Elaine's parents as they pursued their dreams and desire for a better life for their family, George and his family have been enabled to reach the level of achievement and accomplishment that they enjoy today.

THE BELOVED TRADITION

The Story of Bobby and Velma Simmons

"...tragedies, like blessings, can be part of God's plan for a man."

Marion E. Wade[1]

The deep blue field of Virginia's state flag features the state seal of Virginia with the Latin motto, *Sic Semper Tyrannis*—"Thus Ever to Tyrants." The seal depicts a woman standing over the fallen body of a tyrant. Virginians have a long history of fighting valiantly against their foes, including the final major battle of the American Revolutionary War in 1781 and the bloody Manassas battles of the Civil War. Virginians are known for their love of independence and self-determination—and the Simmons are true Virginians.

Bobby and Velma Simmons, the owner/operators of ServiceMaster of Fairfax, Vienna, Leesburg, Prince William

County, and South Riding, Virginia, are quintessential Virginians. They have fought against tyrants that would have rode over others of weaker faith, and they have emerged victorious.

VALUES GROWN ON A FARM

"I was the middle child in a family of nine children," said Bobby. "We were taught to be independent at a young age. We weren't wealthy by any stretch of the imagination, but from the beginning, I remember that I wanted to be an independent businessman. In fact, back then being independent was the most appealing factor of business ownership, and that's still true for me today. At an early age my parents instilled in all nine of us the understanding that we must always do our best at whatever we were doing. We were taught to be optimists. They told us that if we worked hard things would work out for us. We grew up believing we could be successful."

CHURCH AND INSURANCE

The Simmons' involvement with ServiceMaster began in March of 1962 when Velma accepted a job as a church secretary. Bobby was an independent insurance salesman at the time. During an interview for a promotion, Velma was interviewed by the personnel board of the church. It was then that she met Paul Marth, who was the ServiceMaster distributor in the Greater Washington, D.C. area. "All Paul asked me," Velma recalled, "was what my husband did. He was interested in bringing Bobby into the ServiceMaster family from the very beginning." Through Paul's influence Bobby and Velma were introduced to ServiceMaster, and in September Bobby took a position in Paul's business as a technician, where he worked for several years. "When Bob finally decided to go with Paul, we were young and full of enthusiasm," Velma remembered. "It sounded like a great opportunity to us."

Eventually Bobby decided to take the first step toward the independence that he had been groomed for all his life. "I read some of Marion Wade's statements and commentary," Bobby recalled. "He was very strong on being an independent businessman. I wanted my success to depend entirely on my ability and my desire to get ahead. That really appealed to me."

"We were also impressed by the fact that a Christian founded the company," Velma added. "Bob and I have always been very close to the Lord and very involved in our church."

In September of 1965 they made the decision to purchase a franchise in Fairfax, Virginia, a city 30 miles southwest of Washington D. C. The Simmons remember this as an exciting time of learning. Although they didn't know everything that they thought they needed to, they were optimistic and motivated. Bobby decided to continue working part time in Marth's franchise while building his business so that he would be assured of having enough money to survive. In addition, Velma continued in her position at the church and did the books for the business in the evening.

Velma knew that they were standing at a very important threshold in their lives. "We realized that the business could be the means of providing for us and our family in the future." Any doubts that Bobby might have had about starting his own business were erased when he had the opportunity to hear Marion Wade speak. "I wasn't entirely sold on buying a franchise, but once I heard Marion Wade talk about the opportunities, I said, 'Where is the paper? I want to sign up!'"

"We didn't think about things," said Velma. "We didn't analyze everything like young people do today. Like getting married—as soon as I knew that Bobby was the one we just got married. There was no big question or thinking about problems or what we might think would intimidate us. Nothing intimidated us at the time."

Bobby has always maintained a positive attitude about the business and has had the ability to leave the job there at the end of the day. "We locked the door of the office at six o'clock. We didn't put in 80 hours a week. I would say, 'Lord, I have done my best today, and tomorrow is another day.' That is how I faced it if I couldn't get everything done or if things didn't go right during the day. We always had an opportunity to do better tomorrow."

"You Hunt Better When You're Hungry"

When Bobby and Velma began their business, they faced one persistent problem: they didn't have enough customers to meet their financial needs. "I don't recall that we went hungry or missed meals. But it was tight. We didn't consider giving up; we knew that we just had to keep going," Velma admitted.

There were times when they didn't have any customers, and Bobby went out knocking on doors in the snow, trying to get business. "Finally some man felt sorry for him and let him clean his carpets," remembered Velma. Bobby laughed, "You hunt better when you're hungry. If I didn't have any work I would go out and knock on doors."

For the first five years of the business, that was a common occurrence. Even after they hired other employees, they still used this method to generate new customers. Bobby describes their strategy: "If we had a job in a particular neighborhood, we would park a ServiceMaster identified vehicle in the middle of the neighborhood and then go door to door from there. We did this for at least five years."

From the Ashes

In August of 1982, almost two decades after beginning the business, the Simmons were excited to finally have an opportunity to take a "real vacation." Along with their accountant and his wife, they had purchased front-row tickets to the Grand Ol' Opry in Nashville, Tennessee. But before they had a chance to see the performance that was scheduled for that evening, they received devastating news: their business offices had been destroyed by a fire. As they were flying home that night, Bobby remembers the despair that he felt. "I thought, *this is it.* I thought that we had lost everything. That was a pretty hard time. We were ready to just give it up and figured that the Lord was trying to tell us something. In those days every penny added up and was very critical to our business. We had a lot of office equipment and chemicals that were destroyed. People who know me claim that I am very stubborn, but this was a very low point for me. My mother-in-law tried to encourage me by telling me that there would be a silver lining in this cloud, but I told her, 'I just don't see it.'"

As it turned out, their production manager, Bill, had the courage and foresight to ask the firemen to let him into the office so that he could gather up important papers. Several checks that had been left out on the secretary's desk were saved. "They were pretty badly charred but we called each customer, and they gave us a new check. After that we moved into the back of another warehouse for a week or so, and then for the next six months we operated out of a building with no windows until the property owner rebuilt the burned offices. We moved everything that was salvageable to our house, and the children and I dusted smoke off all the files for weeks."

THE SILVER LINING

"From that day forward we have continued to grow," Bobby declared. It was after the fire that Velma came back into the business full time at Bobby's request. "Honey, if we are going to make it," he said, "you are going to have to join me." So she left her position at the bank, and, after having persevered through their great hardship, they began a period of rapid growth. "We had customers who came looking for us after the fire to try and find out where we were and what had happened," Velma stated.

At that point they were doing a combination of both disaster restoration and residential work and were being moderately successful. After the fire they began to concentrate more fully on the disaster restoration business particularly because Bob had always had good rapport with insurance adjusters and partly because the fire had given them firsthand experience—although they don't recommend that as a way to get training.

HELPING OTHERS DEVELOP

Helping people develop has been Bob's pride and joy. One individual he remembers came to him as a young boy right out of high school. This young man was lanky and very quiet, even to the point that he wouldn't talk more than once or twice during the day. But he was a tremendous worker. He moved up through the ranks slowly at first because the Simmons weren't convinced that he had the skills required for a good crew chief. But after time, he proved to be an excellent crew chief. Then he became a production manager and "did a great job with that. Whatever position we gave him he met our expectations and went beyond them. Next he became an estimator and worked with the insurance companies writing estimates. He was great at that. So, we eventually sold him on the idea of buying a franchise of his own. He took that business and built it so well that in a couple of years he decided that running it was too much for him. So he sold it to us and came back into our business as a senior estimator. In 1996 he became a large loss adjuster for a major insurance company." It was this quiet young man, Bill, that had the presence of mind to pull their important papers out of the fire. He started working for the Simmons in 1964 and stayed with them until 1996. Now his oldest son works for them, and he's just as lanky as his dad was and doesn't talk much either.

Bobby has always tried to make everybody realize that they are part of a team effort, not just stand-alone employees. The Simmons have tried to maintain one-on-one relationships with all their employees through the years. They have shunned any management philosophy that didn't see the entire workforce as a team. "We don't see ourselves as big 'corporate officers', and our employees as measly peons. We try to make them feel that they are a part of the reason that we've been successful."

This philosophy has motivated Bobby to make an effort to speak to every employee at some time during the day. At times, he will corner one and ask their thoughts about their job and how management could help them. He wants to know how to make it better for the employee and for the business. "Both parties have to benefit from this relationship," Bobby stated. "I am afraid some of us look at an employee and think, 'how much can he make for me today?' I know we're in business to make money, but I want to share it with my employees or team members as much as I possibly can."

Another element of the Simmons' team-building philosophy is trust. "If you can't trust your employees in your business office, then you can't trust them in a customer's home. I think they realize that we do trust them. We have a 10,000-square-foot warehouse full of people's belongings. All of our full-time employees have a key to that warehouse. If I can't trust them in the warehouse, I am not going to send them into someone's home. We believe that it's very important to show these people that we do trust them."

Not only do the Simmons trust their employees, they also reward loyalty by giving them ServiceMaster stock at their five- and ten- year work anniversaries. ServiceMaster of Fairfax has won the Expert Award on two occasions, and the Simmons know that the employees are the reason for their accomplishments. "We have a reputation for being dependable. The insurance companies and regular customers that we work with know that our employees will get it done and get it done right." And the Simmons love to reward that dependability. Although the way that insurance losses are handled is changing rapidly, they know that there will always be losses to handle and that they will get their share if they continue to produce their product the way that they always have. These days ServiceMaster of Fairfax boasts 32 team members and is one of the top twenty revenue producers in the ServiceMaster Clean organization.

VICTORY OVER ANOTHER TYRANT

In 1999 Bobby was diagnosed with multiple myeloma, a type of cancer that affects the plasma cells and attacks the bones. Although he's been in remission for over a year now, and the outlook is very positive, circumstances were difficult at the time his cancer was discovered.

"Bob's mother had just passed away. We were devastated—we didn't even know what the words *multiple myeloma* meant. Our world was turned upside-down again. Our three children, Kelly, Mark, and Stephen, my sister Donna and her husband Reece, our church friends, and of course, the Lord really helped us. They all lifted us up in an unbelievable way and without them we would have fallen apart. After some investigation, our son told us about a treatment program in Little Rock, Arkansas. Once we had made the decision to go to Arkansas for evaluation, Mike Isakson contacted the franchisees in that area, Bernie and Beverly Wait. These people have become dear friends—we call them our 'adopted family.' They take care of us while we are in Arkansas for treatment. That first day they picked us up at the airport and helped us get acquainted with the area. We ended up being in Little Rock for 14 days…they even had us over for Easter dinner. That was such a wonderful blessing because we had been eating hotel food for 14 days."

Because of Bobby's illness, their son, Stephen, has become increasingly involved with the business and will eventually take it over. "When I walked away from the business with my illness, Stephen stepped in, and he increased the revenue substantially. Knowing that Stephen can make the business grow is a real positive for us. We think that the business is in good hands with him, and we know it will continue to have excellent growth. I want to continue to be involved, to concentrate on consulting and training. Velma will stay in the business and take care of the accounting. But we'll also take the time to pursue other interests, including music and working on the six acres we own and enjoying our grandchildren."

THE PROUD HERITAGE

Historically, Virginians have been known as people who stand by their guns, who pursue independence, and who aren't afraid of facing oppressors in taking a stand for what they believe to be right. Like the Virginians before them, the Simmons have faced difficulty, worked hard, and have carried on the great tradition established by people like Patrick Henry and Robert E. Lee. They have been happy in the pursuit of their goals, and they've loved what they've done. If you asked them if they have suffered much in their quest for independence, they would say, "No!" They believe that God has led them every step of the way, and even though they've had troubled times, they've always known His strength and presence.

BUILDING FROM
THE HEART

The Story of Reece and Donna Conner

*"In building a business...we've got to think
about the other fellow's problems, help him do
his job and even make personal sacrifices if the
job is to be done at all."*

Marion E. Wade[1]

It's an interesting coincidence that Reece Connor
interviewed for his first position with ServiceMaster
on Valentine's Day, 1966. Valentine's Day, the holiday most
associated with the heart, is a fitting day to commemorate
this start in Reece's life. You see, Reece Conner is a man of
great heart.

After his discharge from the Navy in 1963, Reece and his
wife Donna began looking for opportunities for employment. Donna's brother-in-law, Bobby Simmons, had met a
man named Paul Marth at church and had decided that
because of its reputation for integrity, ServiceMaster was a

company with which he could feel comfortable working. Reece knew that he was stuck in a dead-end job, so the thought of working for a company like ServiceMaster was intriguing. At that time Paul Marth was a distributor, and after the interview on Valentine's Day, Reece decided he, too, should become part of the ServiceMaster family.

FROM EMPLOYEE TO EMPLOYER

In those early days, service employees were considered subcontractors. They owned their own truck, chemicals, and equipment and were given a percentage of each job. After three years of working as a service associate, Reece was informed that there had been a change in the laws governing subcontractors. Therefore, he was given three options: 1) he could quit and find another job; 2) he could go to work as an employee for the Master Franchise; or 3) he could purchase his own business. So in November 1969, Reece and Donna Conner bought the service territory that included one-quarter of Arlington County, Virginia. Neither Reece nor Donna had any experience running a business, but Reece was a hard worker, and they knew that buying his own business was better than working for someone else. "At first there was no real attraction to ServiceMaster," they recalled. "It was just a way to get out of a little town and to do better than we had been."

The prospect of leaving Clifton Forge, a small town of only 5,000 residents, was both exhilarating and intimidating for them. Although Reece had traveled some in the Navy, from their perspective, Arlington was a daunting metropolis. It seemed to be filled with highly educated people who were rich and politically powerful. In spite of their apprehensions, Reece and Donna packed up their belongings and their two-and-a-half year old daughter and moved, not knowing what was going to come next. All they had was the trust that somehow they would survive. In the process, they exchanged a comfortable, inexpensive home in Clifton Forge for a crowded little residence that cost three times as much. When

Donna saw the property Reece had rented, she spent the whole weekend crying. At that point, life looked pretty bleak. They didn't know how they were going to make ends meet, and the truth was that they had "zero employees, zero customers, and zero revenue." The one asset—the only asset—that they did have was *heart*.

WORK EXPERIENCE TOO CLOSE TO HOME

It wasn't until Reece and Donna gained firsthand experience with the kind of business they had purchased that they began to get more excited. One morning they looked in the mirror and found that everything in their little home had been covered with soot. They'd had a "puff-back" (when smoke from an oil-burning furnace is released through heater vents rather than the flue) during the night, and it was this experience that really introduced them to what ServiceMaster was all about. Paul Marth, their distributor, wrote a fire estimate for them, and they did the cleaning. It was then that they knew what ServiceMaster could mean in a person's life.

In 1972 Reece and Donna attended their first Service-Master conference in Chicago, Illinois. It was this conference that radically altered their view of what they could accomplish through their business. "For the first time we developed a vision for what was possible," they remember. They watched their peers win awards, and as the recipients of the Marion E. Wade Award accepted their honor, Reece made a heart-promise to himself: "Someday, with Christ's help, I'm going to do that."

The Conners' franchise was transformed almost overnight. Instead of looking at the business as a job or just some little mom-and-pop operation, Reece and Donna knew that they could accomplish something really significant. "We caught the vision, and it has never left."

Marion E. Wade was a key part of their change. His humility and willingness to speak with each franchisee gave them the hope that they needed. They began to see that they, too, could be successful. They understood that two ordinary people with integrity and commitment could accomplish something very extraordinary. They could overcome any obstacle, even the one that they felt most keenly: their lack of a formal education.

"Marion gave us the vision that we could be something. We believed him because he was so down-to-earth, so genuine, and full of sincerity. He actually enjoyed talking with us. We learned from him that his success wasn't something he accomplished on his own but was because he had gathered good people around him."

"CAN YOU HANG ON? ... THE BABIES ARE CRYING..."

Those early years in the business were frantic, hair-raising, and yet exhilarating. The Conners had set up their office in the laundry room of their home, and Donna spent her days chasing their daughters, answering the phone and scheduling appointments for Reece. Sometimes things were so hectic that she was forced to call customers back. Rather than hurting their business, this endeared the Conners to their customers, and for years since many have asked, "How are your baby girls?"

SUPERHERO IN A VAN

One of Donna's responsibilities in the business was to schedule Reece's daily appointments. Reece had bought her a map so that she could become more familiar with the service area. "Here is D.C., here is Alexandria, here is Arlington," he told her. As Donna looked at the map, the cities all seemed so close together—really, they were separated only by bridges—that she proceeded to book his appointments at 15-30 minute intervals. Although the areas were close together geographically, it took a significant amount of time to get across the bridges from one area to another. So, in order to be on time for his appointments, Reece frequently found himself having to change his clothes on the run. "I would put on a shirt and tie real quick and go out and do the estimate. I was like Superman changing clothes in the back of the van."

In 1971 Reece realized that things had to change. He told Donna that he was finally going to move the business out of their laundry room. "I want to get an office and find some employees, and I'm going to run this thing like a real business," he promised. It wasn't long after that that the break they had been waiting for finally came.

One of the Conners' clients was a freelance writer for the *Washington Post*. The client was intrigued as she watched Reece clean her carpet and, at her request, he agreed to be photographed and interviewed. As time went by, however, he didn't hear anything from her, so the incident eventually faded from his memory. That is, until they arrived at church one Sunday morning about a month later. Friends and acquaintances were coming up to Reece, patting him on the back. "I saw you in the paper—congratulations!" they said. The Conners were flabbergasted. Later, when they finally got a copy of the paper, they found that the story about their business was on the first page of the Living In Style section! There were three big pictures of Reece with a caption that read, "No White Tornado ever cleaned like this!" As you can imagine, the phones of all the ServiceMaster franchises in the area rang repeatedly the following day. Their distributor received over 250 calls following the article, and the Conners' business was finally off and running.

PRINCIPLED HEARTS

Even though they worked for highly educated, successful people, the Conners never took advantage of their clients. "We knew that we could have charged them more. We even knew that they had money and would pay whatever we asked. But we just wouldn't do that."

"I could have cheated them," Reece remembers, "but I never wanted to walk out of anyone's house thinking, *Boy, I got them.* It was an honor to God to ask a good price for a good job...and that's what we did. I've never had to look over my shoulder."

The name "*ServiceMaster Clean*" is more than a description of the company's cleaning methods. It's a statement about principles in the heart that drive one's actions. In all of their dealings with their employees and customers, Reece and Donna made it their continual policy to be honest and fair.

"Dealing with people honestly and fairly has its own reward. It gave us a good feeling, *a clean feeling.*" That's the kind of attitude that Marion Wade and the other founders brought into the business: They were men who knew what *ServiceMaster Clean* was all about. It was a state of the heart that naturally worked its way out into relationships with customers and employees. It was reflected in the way that the Conners forged bonds with their staff. An employee who had come from a very rough background once told Reece, "You're the first person in my life who hasn't cheated me." Reece's relationship with this employee was life-changing: Because of Reece's influence, the man moved into a home, got married and adopted his wife's children. The time that Reece has spent with him, training him not only in proper cleaning methods but in character and faith, has made an eternal impact on him.

Reece and Donna Conner are people who have experienced the pleasure of helping other people. "All my life I've tried to help others," Reece remembers. "I love to touch someone else's life...just to be able to help them in some way. You know, I just get a good feeling from that. I have the feeling it is the Lord working through me."

It is good business practice for a man to spend time training his employees. That's commonplace. What's truly amazing though is how much time Reece has spent training his fellow franchisees. Instead of worrying about others taking business away from him, he has always been happy to see a yellow ServiceMaster van from someone else's business driving down the street. "The more that people see our name—no matter whose van it is—the better it is for all of us." It's that generous, far-reaching philosophy that won Reece the respect of his peers.

For the Conners, success isn't measured in dollars. Success is being able to give to people. It's the joy of watching people whom you've helped become successful themselves. "Success is all in the heart," Reece intones. "*Heart* means that you want to work and help others, and you're not doing it for any monetary reward. It is the drive to reach out, to step out, to put aside fear and be willing to make mistakes. It has to do with your inner desires, your drive, your *want-to*. When you have heart you don't know that you're being overlooked or laughed at. You don't know that you're being envied or rewarded. You don't even know when the race is over, and it's not something that you can turn off after 20 minutes." *Heart* is the word that encapsulates the Conners' business philosophy.

What's nice about most people with this heart-driven philosophy is that they don't even know how unique and special they are. The Conners are in this category, and in 1988, Reece realized his dream of receiving the Marion E. Wade Award at the National Convention in Chicago.

LIVING THROUGH A BROKEN HEART

But it was also in 1988 the Conners faced their greatest challenge. Reece had a serious heart attack and had to have major surgery. During the drawn-out, intensely painful recovery period the Conners came close to losing their business. But it was also during this time that they discovered the measure of their peers' love and respect. Friends offered to mortgage their homes to help them; others gave them large sums of money and guaranteed their debts. As Reece faced his illness and the difficulties in the business, his heart for his business almost stopped. "Let's not do this anymore," he told Donna. "It is enough. Let's quit." But now it was Donna's turn to display her heart. It was her time to pull the business through. It was her bravery that kept the business together during those difficult days.

"We found out how unique ServiceMaster is during that time," she remembers. "ServiceMaster is unique because the people in it are unique. It makes me cry to think of all the people who helped us. It would be nice to think that the rest of the world is like this, but it isn't. There is not one person among all our fellow ServiceMaster franchisees that wouldn't help us. I don't think that you can find that anywhere else. This is what makes this company great. We found out what this company was all about because they got behind us and helped us when we needed it."

In 1994 Donna Conner received the *Hang Tough Award* from her distributor. Reece and Donna have since built their business back up and now it's solid again. They both have the "heart" back again, and they realize more than ever that they couldn't have done it without the ServiceMaster family standing behind them. As they look forward to their future and the possibilities that a more relaxed involvement in their business may bring, they can be at peace knowing that they never crossed over the lines drawn in their own hearts.

TRUE REWARDS

The measure of a man's success is often seen in his children's appraisal. The Conners have three children, and their second daughter, Hope, had this to say as she reflected on her parents and their lives in ServiceMaster: "You gave a job to your daughter, but ended up giving her a life lesson in experience. My involvement with ServiceMaster has taught me about business, relating to people, professionalism, maturity, integrity, how to persevere, and how to get what I want in life rather than waiting for someone else to give it to me." As

Hope watched her parents struggle through the hard times, she learned priceless lessons. She watched her parents overcome the disadvantages in their lives, particularly during the difficult circumstances. As a result she can say, "I don't think there is anything I can't do, because I have watched them."

Reece and Donna Conner have come a long way since the days when he would leave the house in the morning with less than a dollar in his pocket and hope that some nice customer would offer him lunch. They've grown past the days when they couldn't hear their customers' phone calls because the babies were crying. They've serviced the homes of great politicians and built and then rebuilt a solid business that now produces high levels of revenue. They've watched their daughters grow into responsible women, two of whom are also involved in ServiceMaster businesses. But in all of this, they haven't lost the one thing that sets them apart from the everyday entrepreneur: They haven't lost the heart that believes that if they work hard, treat people with dignity and conduct their business honestly, that the God they trust will care for them. To the Conners, ServiceMaster isn't just a cleaning company; it's a "way of life" that began with the founders and cascades down like a waterfall through the four corporate objectives. It's obvious that what Reece and Donna may have lacked in formal business education has been more than made up for in humility, service, and dedication.

Rx: CAREGIVERS

The Story of Skip and Mary Ann Fryling

*"We all need to be nurtured.
In the firm, it is the responsibility of
leadership to see that it happens."*
C. William Pollard[1]

Registered nurses (RNs) are people whose vocation it is to care for others. They work to promote health, prevent disease, and help patients cope with illness. They are people whose lives are focused on making others' lives better. Even though just half of the Fryling team is trained in nursing (Mary Ann is a registered nurse), the desire to care for and nurture others has transfused their entire business. For the Frylings, there's nothing more important than nurturing their employees through relationships that help them achieve their personal goals. The Frylings are not only employers, they are caregivers.

DOORS OPEN AT AN ICE RINK

Skip Fryling had his first exposure to ServiceMaster in 1970. As a member of an amateur hockey team, Skip would habitually sit next to John Emmons on the bench. Over time, a relationship was formed, and as it sometimes happens after a game, the topic of conversation would turn to work. At the time, Skip was employed as a commissioned salesman for a large corporation. Although his job was steady and secure, he was frustrated by the fact that he couldn't control the delivery of the goods that his customers had ordered. He was making sales but losing some commissions because the parent corporation wasn't delivering the goods as they should. He longed to have his own business, to be the one on whom his success depended.

It was during one of these conversations that John Emmons, who was a distributor for ServiceMaster, asked Skip if he had ever considered getting into the cleaning business. For Skip, the "cleaning business" consisted only of a mop and a bucket. "We're not really like that," John informed him. "Come by and visit my operation sometime. Who knows? Perhaps we might interest you in buying a franchise."

As Skip and Mary Ann sat down together with John Emmons and began to discuss the ins and outs of purchasing a disaster restoration license, they were impressed with the sincerity and integrity that they saw. John Emmons and his partner, Bob Fallon, had sterling reputations in the town, and Skip thought that these were the kind of people with whom he wanted to be associated. He knew that they were religious, and he viewed this distinction as a plus. Like them, he too believed that the golden rule of treating others with respect and dignity was the way to go. But at the end of the meeting, as Skip considered that he had twin daughters who were less than a year old and another child on the way, he hesitated to put his family in such jeopardy. He knew that pursuing his dream of owning his own business would mean that the family would lose their health insurance, and that was very troubling to him. It was then that Mary Ann stepped forward and reassured him: "Skip, you have always wanted to be in business for yourself. Let's give it a try." So, in the fall of 1971, they signed the papers, bought the license, and took what to them was a huge chance by opening a new business in Scituate, Massachusetts.

Needless to say, some members of the Fryling's family weren't as enthusiastic as Skip and Mary Ann about their prospects. Their parents wondered how they would survive operating a fledgling cleaning business. Questions about the wisdom of giving up their health insurance right before the birth of a third baby were asked. But deep within Skip's heart was the desire to test his limits…to see what he was capable of. He longed for the opportunity to grow and to provide his employees with the same opportunity to grow as well. He wanted to have the chance to treat employees the way that he wanted to be treated, to provide them with the kind of workplace environment that he had always wanted. *What would happen,* he wondered, *if workers knew that they were cared for and given the freedom to reach their full potential?*

Although Mary Ann had been working in a hospital in Boston, she decided that it would be prudent to devote herself principally to their business during the day. She found this new position very challenging simply because her training had been in caregiving, and she had never learned how to keep books for a business. In addition, in order to supplement their income, she worked in the evening for local doctors, who kindly offered to deliver their third child, another daughter, without charge.

TEARS AROUND THE PICNIC TABLE

The business was started in their home, with Mary Ann overseeing the office responsibilities, and Skip doing the sales and production. Their first base of operations was a picnic table that the family used to dine on. Every morning around that table, Skip and Mary Ann and their first few employees would meet to go over the schedule, allocate assignments and start the day.

Skip devoted himself to acquiring jobs and then would frequently perform the work as well. He wasn't always successful in clinching every deal, but wasn't afraid to fail. He tried to learn from his mistakes and to avoid making them again. Mary Ann mastered the office procedures and learned how to oversee the finances.

They will both acknowledge that those first few years were tough. Mary Ann admits that more than once tears were shed, particularly when they seemed to be meeting their sales goals but were still unable to meet all their obligations or even buy groceries. "I rode around in a little yellow truck," Skip remembers, "and we were happy if we put food on the table."

It was during these difficult first years that they received a lot of needed assistance from the ServiceMaster home office. Dan Kellow spent time with them going over the business, visiting with their accountant, and helping them to reorganize. He saw that they were really suffering because the money just didn't seem to be coming in, and so on a number of occasions he sat with them and went over the business operations with a fine-tooth comb. Skip and Mary Ann were struggling financially and were forced to borrow to achieve the necessary cash flow during periods of expansion and growth. Between the advice they got from Dan Kellow and the help they received from the local bank, they were able to make it through those difficult first years.

It was during this time that Skip was asked to be on the board of his local bank. He chuckles as he recalls how humorous he thought the idea was. "I thought that they asked me to be on the board because I owed them so much. I just figured that they didn't want to lose track of me." But as time went on, Skip and Mary Ann could see light at the end of the tunnel. Because both of them were hard workers, they were able to persevere and to eventually watch their business prosper.

Two Talents Merging Together

Skip knew how to acquire jobs and how to relate with the public, and he enjoyed the hard work that his position afforded him. Mary Ann, on the other hand, was still a nurse at heart. The corporate objective of helping people develop blended nicely with the philosophy of her chosen profession. She relished the opportunity of caring for others. She loved helping the employees and giving them the chance to grow into individuals fulfilling their potential. Both Skip and Mary Ann believe in promoting employees from within the company rather than hiring someone on the outside, thereby affording their workers opportunities that they might never have had otherwise.

For instance, one employee, Jimmy McCarthy, came to them straight out of high school. Although he had limited work experience, the Frylings believed that if they gave him direction and cultivated his skills, he would become a valued employee for them and find fulfillment for himself. In the beginning Jimmy started out as a crew assistant, helping in general manual labor. Although he spent every summer helping in his family's painting business, he also enjoyed his work with ServiceMaster and looked to the Frylings to help guide him in his career. It wasn't too many years before he became a crew chief, overseeing others and teaching them the skills they needed to become good employees. Then the time came for him to make a significant move up. The need for an assistant manager and estimator was evident, and Skip and Mary Ann thought that Jimmy was the right one for the job. He was glad that they thought so highly of his potential, but was fearful that he wouldn't be able to do the job properly. "I don't have the paper skills, and I don't know how to do the job," he objected. But in the end they persuaded him that they would train him and that he could be successful. Indeed, Jimmy had found his niche. He is now 33, engaged to be married, and has worked for the Frylings for 15 years. He's had the opportunity to travel to conferences and has experienced the very benefits that Skip and Mary Ann longed to provide for employees. The Frylings nurtured him and gave him room to fulfill his own potential, and now he's wearing a suit to work, overseeing a large part of their business.

How to Grow Profitably

The Frylings believe that their philosophy of caring for others is the key to their business's profitability. "I've never changed my initial belief that employers should treat their employees the way that they want to be treated," Skip asserts. "I want to be an encouragement to my employees. Even if I have to correct them I always want to remember that they are individuals, and I never want to demean them in any way. I believe that if you pay them well and treat them well, you'll be able to retain them." It's probably due to this philosophy that the company has such a high rate of employee retention. Among their office staff, the average length of stay is 15 years.

Mary Ann utilizes her nursing skills by acting as the counselor for the company. Whenever anyone has a problem, whether it is a marriage problem or even just a question of how to manage one's finances, they go to Mary Ann. They know that they'll get sound advice and that their concerns won't be spread around. At a time when she could slack off in her involvement, every employee knows that Mary Ann's door is always open.

In addition, Mary Ann functions as the social director and keeps track of the employees' personal lives. She's personally involved with the families of each employee and knows who is having babies and who is going on vacation. Whenever an employee takes his or her family on a vacation, Mary Ann makes sure that they have a little extra money for the children to spend. Recently when one of the crew chiefs was embarking on his first real vacation, she gave an extra $50 in Disney Dollars for the kids. Mary Ann, who loves to give and deeply cares for others, is rewarded with simple little notes of thanks from the children.

As employers, Skip and Mary Ann are very involved socially with their workers. They've taken them, along with their families, on fishing trips and whale-watching excursions. They believe that it is because they treat their employees in this way that they've never been strapped for help when they need it. "If we need four volunteers, we get four volunteers."

SUCCESS MEANS HELPING PEOPLE GROW

The Frylings define success as "helping people grow to achieve their personal goals." Even though they have received the highest honor that ServiceMaster bestows, they still don't view that as the best measure of their accomplishments. Although it was a great honor for them to receive the Marion E. Wade Award in 1996, for them that's not really what success is all about. Mary Ann believes that "success is not a destination, it is a journey." This never-ending journey has to do with pressing on, never sitting back, encouraging others to develop. It's the constant striving forward to help others be all that they can that defines their accomplishments. And so, after winning the Marion E. Wade Award, the Frylings took 25 employees and their managers and crew chiefs for a cruise in Boston harbor for the night. "This isn't mine and Mary Ann's award," Skip told the group. "This is your award. And if it wasn't for you folks we wouldn't have received the award. Just because our name is on it doesn't mean it's our award."

At the beginning of the business the task was to survive. Now the task is to help others achieve their goals and to develop. Skip has had to learn to trust others, to delegate, and to believe that if he gives people a chance to succeed, they will. That was a very difficult lesson for him because the business had, in some ways, become the sole focus of their lives. For instance, even though they would try to talk about other interests at the dinner table, inevitably the conversation always got around to the company. As time went on, even their children, who were employed in the business, would talk about it.

RELATIONSHIPS DEFINE WHO THEY ARE

The Frylings believe that the relationships they have with employees, customers, and their peers are the most important facet of their business. "You'll be successful in this business if you treat people well in every relationship. That includes how you handle them and how you respond to their problems," Skip believes. "If they have a problem with a job, and I can't reach them during the day, I'll call them from home at night. Communication is the key to maintaining relationships, and we make it our policy to try to be good communicators." Skip is concerned about the trends toward computerization because he's afraid that the relationships he so cherishes may weaken; but he also recognizes that the business world is changing and that they'll have to change with it.

REAPING TENFOLD REWARDS

The Frylings have worked hard for many years to achieve their level of success. They've learned that success doesn't happen overnight—that it's a journey that entails a lot of hard work. They've experienced the truth that only entrepreneurs know: You sink or swim by your own capabilities and hard work.

But it hasn't only been hard work. They've enjoyed the blessings that have accrued to them and their family. Their daughters have had the opportunity of seeing commerce from both sides: as an employer and an employee. The girls have met the CEOs of large corporations and have worked side-by-side with janitors. They've traveled extensively with their parents and have garnered the breadth of wisdom that comes from interaction with diverse peoples. They've learned from their parents to respect others, especially those who may not be in the same sphere as themselves.

"We've tried to teach our daughters to respect others. When it comes to the business, if you treat your employees with the respect and dignity they desire, you'll reap the rewards tenfold." That has certainly been true in their experience.

In the 30 years the Frylings have been in business, in both disaster restoration and commercial services, Skip and Mary Ann haven't wandered far from her training as a caregiver. They've helped their employees and customers cope with difficult circumstances; they've sought to encourage the development of personal skills; and they have been advocates for the advancement of those who have had relationships with them. Although Mary Ann might have thought she was leaving her chosen profession in 1971, in reality she never did. It's just that now her husband has joined with her in it.

STANDING ON THE SHOULDERS OF GIANTS

The Story of Jeff and Julie Strong

> *"…there is no room for half-hearted indifference."*
> Marion E. Wade[1]

Nineteen sixty-seven was a historic year for the Canadian people as a whole and for Ross Strong's family in particular. While the rest of his countrymen celebrated Canada's one-hundredth anniversary of confederation, Ross Strong went to a franchise trade show where he learned about the business opportunities available with ServiceMaster. As a fireman, he was looking for a chance to push the limits of his strength and vitality, so he purchased a license and started a residential cleaning and disaster restoration business in his home.

Jeff, Ross's eldest son, remembers those early years as very trying. "The family lived in a small bungalow. The business was located there, also. It was pretty difficult financially, especially after my dad quit his job as a fireman. Mom and Dad invested everything they had in the business…and with three kids in the home it was pretty tough." After living through those difficult early days, Jeff was convinced that he didn't want any part of small business ownership.

Ten years later, by the time Jeff had reached his early twenties, the family business had grown and was consistently profitable. Ross had even branched into a janitorial business that was developing.

"Thanks, But No Thanks"

One evening Ross invited Jeff to join him at the kitchen table. "Jeff," Ross said, "this janitorial business would be a good opportunity for you, and you should be involved in it. It will look after you down the road. You have this much money that comes in," Ross explained, "and this much goes to employees, this much for chemicals, this much for fees, and the rest is for you. This is a good business." But Jeff had seen the other side of small business ownership, too. He remembered the complaining customers, the demanding insurance adjusters, and he believed that being an entrepreneur just wasn't for him. "Thanks, but no thanks," was his response.

Three months later Ross asked Jeff and his girlfriend, Julie, to join at him the table. "Jeff, Julie," he explained, "this is a good business. This much comes in from revenue, this much goes out for fees, chemicals, the government, and the rest is for you. You need to be involved." But, being a small business owner still wasn't all that attractive to Jeff. He was aware of all the financial pressures, and he knew that his dad was working seven days a week. There wasn't any attraction for him. Again, Jeff said, "No thanks, Dad."

At that time Jeff was actually working for another ServiceMaster owner in a different company, cleaning the inside and outside of buildings and factories. Julie was working at a bank. They had good steady incomes and weren't interested in buying into all the problems that came with business ownership.

But, three months later Ross said to Jeff yet again, "Come and sit at the table and let's talk. This is a good business, and it is a good future for you." Ross then pointed out that Jeff was already working for another ServiceMaster company seven days a week, ten hours a day. His mom, Kathleen, and dad reminded him, "You are already doing this for another firm. You need to at least try this because you seem to have the gas tank and the energy level necessary to make this go." This time, Jeff finally acquiesced and said, "Well, I guess so."

Jeff took the reigns of the janitorial business in March of 1976. Then, in September of 1977, Jeff and Julie were married, and a strong business team was built on the dynamic foundation his parents had already forged. Julie continued to work in a bank during the day and did all Jeff's bookkeeping and payroll matters at home at night. She had gone to business school for two years and had some business background, so her knowledge was a great help. As Ross's and Jeff's businesses continued to grow, Julie started working full time for both of them. "Dad always had someone to do his clerical work, but I did his books," Julie recalled. But after Jeff's business really began to take off, she had to give that up and start looking after their business alone.

"When we first took over the business we had about seven or eight employees," Jeff remembers. "I would do sales during the day, deliver the checks, and do customer service. Every night I would check the crews. Then, on the weekends, I would do floor work. Julie did all the clerical work and administration at home in one of our little rooms."

STRENGTHS AND WEAKNESSES

Jeff remembers that the most difficult part of his job was getting new accounts. Because of his youth he had a great capacity for labor and a lot of energy, but his age was a factor that worked against him. "I was intimidated because I was so young. I was only 20. I didn't think that I would ever be able to sell a job," Jeff admitted. "That was my problem. I thought that potential customers wouldn't take me seriously or give me the time of day because I was so young. I was afraid of the customers, and I didn't want to make that phone call to look for a new job. I remember that clearly now."

Thane MacNeill from ServiceMaster of Toronto encouraged Jeff to get a box and fill it with cards that had a business name and contact person written on each card. He told Jeff to call each business once every three months. Thane said the only way Jeff could get over his fear of calling was to force himself to make calls consistently. "Start making your calls," he instructed Jeff. "You will overcome your fear." So Jeff started phoning customers and kept going at it until he felt comfortable with that aspect of his work.

"One of the first big jobs that I sold was at Smith, Klein, and French," said Jeff. "When I first went there, the building was only a hole in the ground with a construction trailer nearby. I worked and worked and worked all through the construction phase of that building to convince the overseer of the project that he should give me the account. That was in 1980, and the building was to have 50,000 square feet of office space. I think I badgered him enough," Jeff smiled, "that in the end he gave me a chance to clean the facility. That was my biggest customer, and it was an uphill battle to get that account. It was a reputable business with a good name, and through them I was able to attain credibility in my market."

One of Jeff's strongest assets is his tenaciousness. He worked hard to sign up new accounts, and nothing bothers him more than losing a customer. "That really troubles me. It used to take me months to get over it. I try now to come to grips with that side of the business without being so disturbed by it," says Jeff. His wife Julie has been an excellent help for him during such difficult times. She encourages him by reminding him that these things just happen in business—it's just part of the life of a business. Still it's a struggle for him: "I can't figure it out. I know that I take it far too personally."

PURSUING EXCELLENCE THROUGH INVESTING IN LIVES

The pursuit of excellence begins as the Strongs strive to do each little thing right. Jeff believes that if they keep working with that goal in mind, they will achieve their goal of excellence by the end of the day. "I'm pretty tough on myself," Jeff confessed. "I think that's the reason that we've been successful. I try to get the most out of everybody, including myself. We work with real average people, but I keep coaching them and trying to get more and more out of them. It's this pursuit of excellence that's made us successful." Although Jeff recognizes that many of his employees appear to be ordinary laborers, he knows that they are the groundwork upon which his business has been built, and he values each and every one of them for their special contribution.

Has Jeff's philosophy worked? In December of 2000, the Strongs hosted their company's annual Christmas party. On that night they gave away three 15-year pins, as well as several 10- and 5-year ones. The Strongs believe that if they treat their technicians properly while giving them the opportunity to make the extra income they need, their employees will stay with them. "Sure, we focus on the customer and try to pursue excellence and provide a good service for them, but we also try to look after our cleaners. If we do that, we find that they, in turn, look after our customers. Caring for our employees provides longevity—both with our clients and our cleaners."

CLEANING MACHINES

The Strongs value their employees and know that even though one may start as a technician, he might very well end up a manager. Manny, a Portuguese man who came to work for the Strongs more than 15 years ago, is a case in point. He started out cleaning floors part-time for the business, and then, eight years ago, became one of their managers. Manny is now an operations manager with a territory of his own. He's also brought in other friends and relatives who are now supervisors and working in management.

When Manny first came into the business, he was already employed in a textile factory making clothes. He worked 10 hours a day at the factory, then went home, quickly ate his dinner, and then went out to clean for four or five hours every night. Jeff remembers that Manny worked like a machine.

About 10 years ago, Manny told Jeff that the firm he was working for during the day was going to close its doors. Although he was an excellent worker, Manny wasn't sure that he wanted the additional responsibility of supervision. But the Strongs had spent enough time with him that they felt Manny had the potential for leadership. They began by giving him more responsibility in the evening. Instead of just cleaning buildings, he was supervising several of them. When the clients began to discover who it was that was working in their building, they started calling him during the day. Jeff then convinced Manny to take on the role of customer service. It wasn't long before Manny had been promoted from a cleaner to a supervisor, then to a customer service manager, and finally, to an all-round manager. "He's able to deal with cleaners and customers and payroll and quality issues. Because he is fluent in Portuguese and English, he's a real help to us."

"We have many employees who are fluent in both Spanish and English. But we also have many who aren't fluent in English because most of our employees are from Central or South America. One employee, Carlo, is from Italy. He's been with us over 15 years. His wife and his sons have worked for us, too, cleaning buildings. It's very nice to see that we are able to provide work for this family. They are honest and reliable people who are faithful, hard workers." The Strongs know that their business is built on the strength of each employee—employees whose dedication and work ethic are a testimony to their character. Although this work force might be denigrated by some, the Strongs think that they are among the titans of business.

Another one of the giants in ServiceMaster Contract Services of Mississauga, Ontario is the Strong's receptionist, Linda. "Linda is the most positive person in the world," Julie boasts. "If a customer calls with a complaint, she has no problem dealing with him. She listens, calms him down, and immediately gets a hold of someone to make sure that the problem is resolved. The first initial voice an irate customer hears on the phone can make a tremendous difference in how a customer is turned around. All our clients tell us how wonderful she is and that they are going to steal her," Julie smiles. "But we aren't going to let her go. Linda takes the business to heart. She handles managers and employees well and doesn't get mad at anyone." She's one of the Strong's giants, too.

22 Opportunities a Month

The contract services business is different from other facets of the cleaning business because there is a greater chance for mistakes to happen. "We are in most of these buildings 22 nights a month, and it is very easy for something to go wrong. The problem we face is training our managers to communicate to our cleaners that even though this is just part-time work for them, it is important work. That's why it's so vital to have good managers and supervisors. After all, a client only notices his janitorial service when a garbage can isn't emptied."

Swift Service

How do Jeff and Julie characterize their business? The one word that describes what they are is *service*. Upon reflecting on the business that they've been able to build, they decided that "immediacy of service" is what they want to be known for. "When a customer calls, it doesn't matter if they have a complaint or if they just want prizes for their golf tournament. We think that the most important task before us is to get to that customer in a matter of minutes. You drop everything and answer the customer's call," Jeff stated emphatically. "You don't want a customer brooding if he has a complaint. If he does, it's only going to get worse. So we try to get to them fast and resolve any problems fast."

LEADERS LEADING TOGETHER

Jeff and Julie have now worked together in the business for 25 years. Together with their two sons, they have built a team that is strong and vital. As of 2000, 245 people were employed at ServiceMaster Contract Services of Mississauga, Ontario, and it was one of the top five janitorial revenue producers. Julie still handles all the administration and bookkeeping, while Jeff focuses on customer retention. Together they are truly a success story, but they recognize that their success stems from the fact that they had a considerable step up on their competition—they were standing on the shoulders of giants. "My mom and dad were pioneers. They put so much effort into the business in those early days," Jeff reminisced. "Julie and I have had bad days and sometimes even bad months, but I don't think we've experienced anywhere near the grief that my parents went through. It's like Mike Isakson has said, 'We are standing on the shoulders of giants.' Julie and I are fortunate because we were able to stand on the shoulders of these pioneers, these giants of the past."

REALIZING
THE DREAM

The Story of Doug and Cathy Pound

"We should compete with ourselves, never being satisfied, progressing from what we are to what we ought to be, then going on to all that we can be."
Marion E. Wade[1]

Doug Pound, senior vice president of operations for ServiceMaster Clean, has never deviated from his end goal. Whether he was working in ServiceMaster's Conserv (Contract Services) division as a young college graduate, being a regional manager, operating a successful distributorship in California, or overseeing numerous departments within the ServiceMaster Clean family, Doug has been consistently focused on one goal: Realizing his own personal dream by helping others to do the same. For Doug, there's a heartfelt satisfaction that comes from something more than mere monetary success—a satisfaction that flows out of helping others define and achieve their goals and dreams.

Doug's history with the ServiceMaster family has spanned a lifetime, and that's true as well for Cathy, his wife. As a young Wheaton college senior, he had a chance to hear about ServiceMaster from a recruiter, and he recognized that the values he embraced were very compatible with those in the company.

In 1974 Doug had his first introduction to ServiceMaster and the character of the company's leadership. During his interview, Ken Hansen, a past leader of ServiceMaster, contacted the man who was interviewing him and said that Doug should come up to his office immediately. When Doug arrived he was informed by Hansen he had been looking out his office window and had noticed that Doug's car had been dented by a rock thrown out of the gardener's lawnmower. Ken Hansen offered to pay to have the dent repaired. This simple reaction of taking personal responsibility ensuring that Doug and his property would not be harmed in any way made a lasting impression on him. Doug knew that he had found a home in ServiceMaster—a home just like the one he had been privileged to grow up in. Although Doug didn't know it at the time, it was at this same time that his wife-to-be, Cathy, was learning about the character of ServiceMaster on the other side of the country, in a distributorship owned by Kelly Nielson and Dave Grotenhuis, in Santa Barbara, California.

THE ENTREPRENEURIAL CHROMOSOME

If science ever discovers an entrepreneurial chromosome, Doug's family will certainly carry it. As the third of four boys, Doug had many years of experience working in his father's lightning protection business in Chagrin Falls, Ohio. Doug's father was one of ten children, seven of whom went on to become business owners. Entrepreneurial ventures were part of what it meant to be in the Pound family; as Doug says, "It was in the blood."

Doug recalls his early years working with his father in the business. "I learned very early what it meant to be your own boss, to set your own hours. Watching my dad run a business was a very positive experience for me.

"I began working for him when I was about ten. Trucks would come to our home and deliver the ground rods and supplies we needed. I would unpack all these materials and stack them up in the garage. Then, when I was older, I worked during the summer full time installing lightning protection with my father's crews. My father was a hard worker and the best salesman I've ever seen. But he knew how to balance work with pleasure. In the back of his truck he would always carry his golf clubs and his shotgun. After he finished his work, if it was hunting season, or convenient to play golf, he would spend a few hours at his sport. Being able to observe his work ethic and his ability to relax was a very favorable experience for me."

Doug's father passed away in 1997, and he remembers him as being the kind of person that every pastor would want in his congregation. "He would always welcome people into the church. If someone looked lonely, he'd go up and talk to him. In addition, if there was work to be done at the church, like mowing the lawn, my dad would have the whole family out there on Saturday morning. There was a wonderful consistency between his sales ability and his Christian walk. He was the quintessential *people person*. And he was successful. He was able to send all four of his children to good schools, and we never wanted for anything while we were growing up."

THE DREAM UNFOLDS

When Doug joined ServiceMaster, he thought that he would have a middle-management job. Instead, he spent the first few years overseeing several contract service businesses. From 1974 to 1976 Doug worked for ServiceMaster in Chicago, managing a company-owned janitorial business.

Doug remembers his first challenge: "I had no idea what *janitorial* meant. I knew what a custodian was, but I didn't understand the janitorial concept." But Doug was a quick study, and soon he was overseeing more than 100 employees. After successfully mastering his position in Chicago, the company relocated him first to Greensboro, North Carolina, and then to Dallas, Texas.

In 1978 Doug transferred to California and took a position as what was then called a regional manager, overseeing the franchise market in the Los Angeles and San Francisco areas. But the entrepreneurial chromosome would no longer lie dormant, and Doug decided that although he was very happy with ServiceMaster, he wanted to have a business of his own. So in February of 1979, with the guidance of Ken Hansen, he purchased half-ownership in a distributorship in Santa Barbara, California, from Dave Grotenhuis. Kelly Nielson, who owned the other 50 percent of the business, and Doug became friends and associates. "Kelly is a man of great faith and integrity," says Doug. "He was the dreamer, and I was the systems person. I did the financial work and the systems operations, and Kelly did the sales. Although we were very different, our core values were the same. We were honest and forthright. We never questioned whether we were going to do the right thing or not. I've always considered that Kelly was an excellent partner."

Aside from getting a great business partner at the Santa Barbara office, Doug also found a wife. Cathy had worked in the distributorship business for several years, and they were soon married.

Although Doug enjoyed the distributorship, and it was very successful, he soon discovered that there was a difference between merely teaching someone how to run a business and actually doing it. Beginning in 1974 and throughout his time with the home office, Doug had been instrumental, teaching numbers of workshops, but now he found himself on the other end of the spectrum. "All of a sudden one day I was sitting behind a desk and what I'd been teaching became the reality. Once I had to implement what I had been teaching, I realized that I didn't know it as well as I thought I did. That first six months of being in business was a quick course in reality for me. When you teach it, that's one thing; when you do it, that's a whole other deal."

But Doug also saw the opportunity to fulfill his goal as he worked in the distributorship. "We loved being able to help the franchisees realize their dreams. As a distributor, that was our main objective. There was very little discrepancy between what we believed personally and what ServiceMaster people believed about helping others develop. That was a very comfortable environment to work in.

"ServiceMaster has always had a strong emphasis on training that's embodied in the second corporate objective. Over the years I have learned many different skills, but the greatest thrill for me has always been working with people. Helping franchises realize their dreams was what I loved doing then, and it's the same thing I love doing today. I enjoy helping people excel at what they do, develop, grow, and realize their dream."

Helping people develop was the heartbeat of Ken Hansen, too. And because Ken had retired to Santa Barbara, Doug and Kelly enjoyed the privilege of meeting with him regularly. "We were on Ken's prayer list. Every three weeks or so, our names would come up on his list, and he and his wife Jean would pray for us. They had a strong desire to develop everyone they came in contact with. For instance, having dinner with them was quite different than a typical dinner visit. The first thing we would do when we arrived at their home for dinner was sit in the living room and sing. Jean would go to the piano, and everyone would circle around. Sometimes there would be only four or five of us standing there singing, which felt rather strange. Then Ken would read a Scripture or ask one of us if we wanted to quote a Scripture. One night, Ken suggested that we perform a play for his son Kenny (who was developmentally challenged). So, we reenacted the parable of the lost sheep. Jean, Ken's wife, was down the hall baaing like a sheep, and I was reading the passage from Scripture. It was simply amazing." In all areas of Ken's life, he was committed to help people develop.

After the time of singing and Scripture recitation, they would then go over to Ken's club for dinner. "Ken must have known I felt uncomfortable praying in public, because he called on me every time. He knew I felt uncomfortable about it, and he wanted to help me develop."

Hanging On to the Dream
through a Nightmare

In 1985 Doug and Kelly took on a third partner, Ed Brown. Ed had been a close friend of Doug's for many years in the ServiceMaster family, and the new alliance seemed headed for success. This was not to be.

On August 23, 1986, Doug and Ed decided to take their sons on a fishing trip to Page Lake, near the Grand Canyon. Doug and Ed loaded up their gear in the company's Cessna 172 as they and their boys, Michael and Aaron, anticipated a fun time together. At dusk, as they headed towards their destination, they were concerned about heat lightning they saw in the distance and decided to land at the Grand Canyon airfield to check the weather. Upon takeoff the plane was suddenly pulled into a downdraft that came up over the mountains at the end of the runway. Doug remembers the events of that tragic day. "As we took off we got caught in a downdraft and slammed into two trees about 35 feet in the air. We were traveling at about 65 miles per hour at the time. Instead of clearing the trees we hit them. Tragically, Ed and his son, Aaron, were killed upon impact. My son Michael, who was 7 years old, ruptured his stomach. I was thrown out the front window in my seat. When I woke up sometime later I was in the brush with a broken right wrist and two broken legs. My right ear had been nearly torn off."

As Doug laid there he could hear the sound of Michael's moaning. Then a miracle happened. "I saw light from a flashlight. I yelled out, and a man and his grandson who were out spotting elk found us. Providentially, they had gotten up from their dinner and taken a ride over to the airport to look for elk. As they were walking, they saw the wing of the plane at just about the same time as I yelled down to them. If they had not come by, both Michael and I would have died. They contacted Search and Rescue immediately, and Michael was airlifted to the hospital at Flagstaff." Both Doug and Michael spent a couple of weeks in Flagstaff before being able to return to their home and family in California.

Although Doug and Cathy had always known about values and family spirit in ServiceMaster, it was during this terrible time that they really experienced them. "The number of ServiceMaster people that came to help us was amazing. Kelly called Ken Hansen, and together they went down to see my wife Cathy. Aside from praying with her, they asked her what they could do to help her practically. They helped her map out a way to get from Santa Barbara to Flagstaff. Bob Groff, a dear friend who was a distributor in Seattle at that time, came down to our distributorship business and stepped in with help right away. When I finally came home from the hospital, I was in a wheelchair, and he even helped get me situated." Two months prior to this, when Bob's wife, Sue, and daughter were in a serious car accident, Doug had had the opportunity to go to Seattle and be a tremendous help to Bob, thus freeing him to attend to his family. "That's what it means to be part of the ServiceMaster family. We don't just say that we care for each other; when the chips are down we come through."

Doug's franchisees were very flexible. Because Doug was unable to travel or even go into the office for weeks, his franchisees made the trip to Santa Barbara. This was great therapy for Doug, and their willingness to be flexible touched him.

EXPANDING THE DREAM

In 1995 Doug and Kelly decided to sell their distributorship back to the home office. Doug chose to join the staff there, while Kelly took this as an opportunity to retire. Soon after Kelly's retirement his wife, Connie, was diagnosed with breast cancer. Retirement offered Kelly the freedom to care for Connie and their family. Kelly and Connie's strength and unwavering faith continues to be a testimony to others.

Although Doug might say that he doesn't have a true entrepreneurial spirit, he has a very strong desire to help those who do. As senior vice president of operations he oversees all the information systems, market expansion, finance, and operations departments. Furniture Medic also reports to him.

"As I look back over my life I can see God's hand guiding me all along. Even facing the tragedy of the plane crash has helped me to understand that God has a purpose for me. My history with the company, and even from childhood, has shaped me to be in the position I am today. As someone who managed janitorial accounts, I learned what it was like to try to get 118 people to a job in an evening. I was really under the gun. As a distributor I saw what it was to be an entrepreneur, own my own business, sweat the payrolls, and be in business for myself. What I do now is just the same as I did as a distributor, only on a larger scale. There are more people, more financial concerns, more computers. But it really is just the same. What I did in Santa Barbara with 110 franchises, I do now with 3,500 franchises. This is a real plus for the ServiceMaster Clean family. In fact, over 75 percent of our key managers in ServiceMaster Clean have owned their own businesses. I see that as a factor that makes us very effective. We understand what it means to be in business. We can empathize with our franchisees because we've been there where they are."

REALIZING THE DREAM

Doug remembers a conversation he had with two business partners who were uncomfortable focusing on the profitability of their business. These two men were Christians who believed that it was wrong to try to seek profits. As Doug spent time with them, he saw the change in their attitude as they understood that making a profit is only a means to an end. Because these two men wanted to be very involved in their church, Doug helped them see how a successful business could be the vehicle for that involvement in their eternal concerns.

"Realizing the dream means something different to everyone. Only a very few people in ServiceMaster Clean think that it involves money as an end goal. For most owners, it means living responsibly, honoring God, and helping people develop. That's where the satisfaction comes from. I see it as my goal to help them get there—to help them set out a clear pattern of what they want to accomplish with their business and help them implement their plan. I don't do that personally with each one of them now like I did when I was a distributor. Now I influence the managers and people who report to me. But, in its essence, it's all the same. We want them to enjoy financial success, but the real satisfaction isn't the money. It's the lives we've impacted. It's the people part of our business. A successful business owner can impact people and still use his resources to honor God through those people."

For Doug, ServiceMaster Clean's future will remain focused on people development. "My role is to help my staff develop and realize their dreams. I want my staff to have the right vision for their jobs so they can help the franchisees realize their dreams. At the Academy of Service, when new people introduce themselves and state why they're in business, it's so thrilling for me. I know that if we do our job right we'll be friends with them for another 15-20 years, and they're going to be winning awards and become successful business owners. It's a win-win situation for us all."

If you were to ask Doug about his life, he would candidly say that he thinks he's had it pretty easy. Raised by a mother and father who consistently loved the Lord and taught him to do so, attending a college with these same values, and then moving from there right into ServiceMaster, he can't pinpoint any great obstacles that he's had to overcome. Indeed, if one were to be able to look over the events of his life, it would be obvious that he's been highly successful, not only professionally, but also in his family with Cathy and his sons, Jeff, Michael, Brian, and Nathan. And although it's partially true that he's had it fairly easy, it's also true that he's made right choices all along. He's chosen to live responsibly and to focus his dreams on the success of others. He's chosen to consistently aid others in realizing their dreams…each of these choices being based on his overriding faith and trust in God.

HUMBLE MENTORS

The Story of Wes and Barb Mitchell

"A job has only as much dignity as the man gives it, and the best way to dignify a job is to dedicate your efforts to the glory of God."
Marion E. Wade[1]

There are some people who make you think that you are the most important person in the world. Wes and Barb Mitchell are those kind of people. They are comfortable to be around; they are unassuming and always glad to see you. Although they operate one of the most successful franchises in the ServiceMaster Clean family, their humble demeanor and willingness to shine the limelight on others is exceptional. They have the hearts of teachers, and even though they have one of the largest revenue producing businesses with 120 employees, when you're with them you never feel like they're looking at their watches or just tolerating you. In every way, they've followed in the footsteps of the founders of ServiceMaster.

A REALLY TOUGH INTERVIEW

The Mitchells' association with the ServiceMaster Clean family began in 1971 when Wes was employed in the hospital division of Management Services.

Wes remembers his interview with Ken Wessner. "That was probably the most uncomfortable interview I've ever had. Ken focused his eye on me and said, 'I noticed that you have had several jobs.' He was right. I had been a Naval officer, but after I got out, the longest time I had spent on any one job was one year. I remember saying, 'Mr. Wessner, I have made my decision to come to ServiceMaster. I can't afford to have any more short-term jobs. I'm here for the duration.' I didn't know at that time how many years I would stay…that was almost 30 years ago."

In 1973-74 Wes became the training director for the division of ServiceMaster called Conserv, or contract services. He spent nearly eight years with Management Services (from 1971 to 1979), but when his wife's father became ill, the family needed to move to the Northwest to be with him. There were no Management Services positions open for him in that area, so after a short hiatus from ServiceMaster, Wes became the manager of franchise operations in the Northwest. In this position, Wes oversaw operations from 1980 to March of 1985. Although the job offered the benefit of allowing the family to travel together, eventually the travel became more and more difficult for Barb and their two growing daughters. Barb, who has a master's degree in elementary education, had taught school before the children were born. But now, with children at home, Wes had to travel alone more and more. In addition, he was gone a lot. "Our girls were growing up, and they weren't even asking anymore why daddy wasn't coming home for dinner. It was just a given that he was never there."

TIME TO CHANGE

"After five years I needed a change," Wes admitted. "An opportunity had come along to join with Steve and Laurie Losorwith, who had bought a franchise in the Seattle area a year before from Bob Groff. When Steve and Laurie bought the business, they had 120 percent growth in just one year. Steve was a fantastic salesman, but he was buried under the growth. He actually asked Bob Groff to take the business back! Groff then contacted me and asked if I knew someone who might want to buy into the business."

Barb remembers the day Wes made the decision. "I remember us talking about it, and Wes just blurted out, 'What if that someone is me?' God was leading us then— there is no question in my mind."

"There was a lot that scared me to death about starting a business, but there was so much energy, too. We would go away from our conversations with Steve excited but still very scared. They were talking about buying six new fans!" Barb recalled with humor. "They were going way beyond me, and it was happening very quickly. I just got carried along with the energy of it. But in my own private world there were a lot of questions and fears. Wes and Steve were really something to watch."

So on the day after Easter, April 1, 1985, Wes and Steve signed the papers that would make them equal partners in ServiceMaster of Seattle. Although they were excited, those beginning days were pretty rough. "We didn't have a salary for several months," said Wes. "I remember how hard it had been for us to save money and how easy it was to go through those savings."

ORGANIZED CHAOS

Barb was discussing the new business and the different facets of disaster restoration with her sister Paula when the two of them got the idea that it might be fun to clean other people's crystal. "My sister Paula was a registered nurse, and we looked at each other and said, 'Maybe this is something we could do together.'" This seemingly inconsequential conversation turned into a partnership in overseeing the pack-out division of the fire restoration department which lasted over 14 years.

When Barb and Paula showed up for work they were shocked by what could only have been described as "organized chaos." "Nobody was quite sure of what was going on in the business," Barb recalled. "When we walked in they handed us a mattress to clean. As we looked at the facility, we thought we should have a sink to do the cleaning in. We really didn't even know what a pack-out was at that point."

"I immediately learned that our people weren't trained," Wes soon realized. "For the first year, I felt that we were pulling ourselves up by our bootstraps. I remember the frustration because we didn't have any controls or any systems. I am very system-oriented, and although we tried several systems, we didn't have anything solidly in place. When I first started I didn't know how to do a water job. We were struggling to bring some semblance of order out of the chaos."

THE PRIVILEGE TO SHARE

It wasn't long after the Mitchells got into the business that they knew they needed help. They contacted Gerry Farrelly, the owner of a franchise in San Diego, California, and who, with the help of his employee, Phil Fitzpatrick, ran a successful disaster restoration business.

Barb recalls their influence: "I think that I became more at ease with the situation when Phil Fitzpatrick, Dave Mowry (another franchisee from Los Angeles), and Gerry Farrelly spent time with me. I talked one on one with Phil for hours and hours and hours, and the more I learned, the more I felt that I could handle the demands of the job. I learned that there were ways I could work on setting up this business, there were answers to my questions. Part of the training was just picking Phil's brain. I learned so much. I took copious notes. I finally had something in writing on the pack-out process. We were desperate, and we really wanted to learn. Phil gave us quite an education."

"We owe an awful lot to Dave, Gerry, and Phil for the help they gave us. They never looked at their watch. They took the time to sit down and say, 'This has worked well. You'll find this in the textbook, but here is how it really works.' They weren't too busy to answer any of our questions," Barb stated with gratitude. "These people were very important in our journey."

Wes joined Barb in remembering the influence these men had on them. "We've made it a hard-and-fast rule that if anybody calls and says they want to come and spend time with us, we always make time for them. We believe sharing is not only our responsibility, but also our blessing and our privilege."

Bob Groff, their distributor, was also very supportive of the Mitchells. "On one occasion Bob went to Los Angeles to learn about computers so that he could help us use one in our business," Wes said. "Bob never tried to tell us how to do something he hadn't done. He was always looking for ways to support us without getting in our way or stymying our growth."

TRAILBLAZING IN DISASTER RESTORATION

The Losorwiths and the Mitchells decided that they wanted to excel in only two areas of the on-location business: disaster restoration and commercial services. "We would do residential services if someone put a gun to our head," Wes jokingly remembers.

"Concentrating on disaster restoration was counter to the prevailing wisdom. We were taught that we should try to have a good balance of business instead of seeking to concentrate on one area only. We were also told that we shouldn't grow too fast. We knew we were violating these principles, but we believed that we had a good business plan and that it was the right thing to do."

Their instincts were right. In 1988 they won the Marion E. Wade Master Award for the highest standards of excellence, growth, and stability.

The partnership between the Mitchells and the Losorwiths was a very successful one. "We couldn't have accomplished what we did in this business if it weren't for Steve," Barb testified. The Losorwiths' partnership with the Mitchells lasted until 1994, when the Mitchells bought out Steve's share of the business. Steve then went on to join the ServiceMaster Clean home office.

ELEMENTARY EDUCATION

"School teaching definitely prepared me to work in the business," Barb intoned. "Our number-one priority was to see people as individuals and never as a group. People don't all learn at the same level, either. My training in education really prepared me for that. Paula and I never did a training session with our employees that was merely, 'Okay, it's 7:00 a.m., so let's listen up. We've got some stuff to cover now, and we have to get through it in one hour.' Instead, my sister and I would put on skits and organize games. We were pretty successful in getting our message across. It was fun for me to be able to do this. I taught primary grades, so I knew I didn't have to be a brain surgeon to get a point across. Not that I would treat the employees as children, but you need repetition, and you need to make it fun, and then zero in on each person. Training was the number-one priority. Then when our department hit a significant revenue mark in sales, we came up with quite a party that everyone looked forward to."

HUMILITY FROM THE TOP

The Mitchells recall one wedding that they attended where Ken Hansen, the chairman of ServiceMaster, was seated at their table. Also seated at the table was a young couple who were obviously very impressed with themselves and their employment. They inquired into Mr. Hansen's employment, and he replied humbly, "I work for a cleaning company." He didn't bother to add that he was the chairman of the board of a multimillion dollar corporation. To him, it wasn't important to try to impress people or put on airs.

On another occasion, during a dinner meeting with Mr. Hansen at a restaurant, a waitress spilled a whole tray of food by their table. "By the time I realized what was happening Ken Hansen was already down on the floor picking up all this stuff," said Wes. "He was helping clean up the mess. Needless to say, all the employees in the restaurant were very impressed. I remember that later the waiters came to the table, and one of us said, 'You probably don't know this, but the man who cleaned the carpet for you is the chairman of the board of a Fortune 500 company'. Ken was so service-oriented," Wes said. "He was very intense, but he was very humble. He was a really impressive man."

THE WORDS AND THE MUSIC HAVE TO FIT TOGETHER

During the time that he was involved in conducting training for ServiceMaster in the Con-Serv division, Wes remembers that he felt uncomfortable with the fact that they opened every meeting with prayer. "I remember feeling like I was forcing my religion on others."

On one occasion, Ken Wessner came to him and said, "Don't ever make any excuse for your faith in Jesus Christ." "That one statement had an incredible impact on me because I realized that he was totally right. He just said, 'Don't make excuses, live the life, and be an example.'"

Wes isn't shy about declaring his beliefs today. "Honoring God in all we do is at the top of the pyramid in our business," he states unblushingly. "Our people know it, and even those who are not Christians know and appreciate it. Honoring God starts with the life that I live. It goes down to the little things. How we treat our people is important, of course, but it is also that I won't allow anyone to tell any 'white lies.' Our receptionist can never say that one of us is not in when we are here."

"We emphasize honesty. I pay for postage stamps and chemicals. Those are small things for me to do, but I want to honor God in everything. Other people have a much higher standard for us than we do for ourselves, so we have to be very careful. *The words and the music have to fit together.* We still start our meetings with prayer, even though our staff has grown in size. I don't know what they say about me," Wes said boldly, "it really is unimportant. This is our business, and we have to set the standard. Bringing glory to God has been our prayer from the very beginning. I know that sounds kind of Pollyanna or pious, but it's the truth. And I think that our people are happy—at least that's what those who visit our business say about us."

Barb knows the sacrifices they've made to conduct business in a uncompromising manner. "It's not always popular. There might be a way to make a lot more money if we did certain things, but we aren't going to do them. We take responsibility for jobs that go badly. We are going to do the right thing, and we are going to accept the responsibility when it is ours, even if that means legal entanglements. We are not going to play games. We are not going to compromise. The only time it makes any sense to take a stand, to have morals and a testimony, is in the tough times when it's so easy to compromise."

Through the years, the Mitchells have had the privilege of humbly training many employees and watching them develop. One woman came to them originally on a part-time basis. In many ways, she didn't appear to be the kind of person who was going to excel in the business world. She had come out of a very degrading family situation and had a terrible self-concept. Her confidence was so poor that on one occasion, when the receptionist wasn't in and the Mitchells asked her if she could answer the phones, she said she just couldn't.

Soon, though, they discovered that she was making all her crew chiefs look good. "Don't forget this, did you do this, make sure you take care of this," she would remind them. It wasn't long before she became a crew chief herself. She eventually became the Mitchells' production coordinator and then their estimator.

Now, after 14 years under their tutelage, this woman has just left them for a job in the insurance industry. "She was incredibly sharp, but never had much of an opportunity to grow. She had always been beaten down by people who didn't think much of her. She is now a person who would say that she can accomplish anything...and she probably could."

The story of this woman's growth isn't just a fluke. It's because of the way that the Mitchells have conducted their business—not only with their entry-level employees, but also with their managers. For example, Wes had made it a practice to meet with his department heads on a weekly basis. He called this the M.O.R.T. meeting, which stands for Management Operations Round Table.

"We saw a great need to communicate with one another and share. All of the general managers, plus Mike Mack, our chief operating officer, and Dan Olson, our chief financial officer, and myself get together. We talk about sales, marketing, and bring everyone up to date. We also meet once a month with all of our management people for our Rolling Quarter Review. We set up an open-book style of management. Every division head gets their own financial statements, and they talk about their numbers for the previous month. I made a commitment," Wes continued, "to never embarrass anyone in these meetings, but if the numbers embarrass them, that is not my problem."

Barb remembers these meetings as sometimes encouraging and other times very difficult. "We cheered when other departments did well. But without the Rolling Quarters meetings, managers could have said, 'It wasn't my fault.' So we gave our department heads the control they needed. It is amazing to see how this control makes a difference. They go from being a victim to taking control and asking, 'What are we going to do, and how we are going to do it?' They had to make the decision if they wanted to buy equipment because the cost came directly out of their division. For instance, after the recent earthquake in Seattle, the coordinator of the water department wanted to buy more equipment. He realized that his financials would be affected by that. The cost of this new equipment was going to come out of his operating revenues for that month, so it wasn't a flippant decision he made. If your people don't have ownership," Barb wisely stated, "they can't participate in management."

SEARCHING FOR A NEW FIELD TO SERVE IN

During the last year, Wes has been working on his transition plan out of ServiceMaster of Seattle. Although Barb and her sister Paula retired in 1999, any future transition won't spell the end of the Mitchells' humble mentoring ministry.

"I think that our biggest struggle is that we are waiting to see how God wants to use us now. It's not bad to travel and learn to play golf, but we want to know what else He would like us to do. Some options have come up in short-term missions that really appeal to us."

For those who have been privileged to know Wes and Barb, it isn't much of a leap to think of them humbly teaching and serving on a foreign field. After all, they've been doing that all their lives close to home.

GENUINELY EFFECTIVE LEADERS

The Story of Bob and Claire Knapp

*"We bear witness to our love and obedience by
the type of service we give others."*
Marion E. Wade[1]

In 1980, Lorne Dillon was a salesman for one of
ServiceMaster's main competitors, Pro-Chem. As
Pro-Chem's regional representative, it was his job to try to
convince owners of carpet cleaning businesses of the superi-
ority of Pro-Chem's products. He visited all the businesses in
his five-state area, ServiceMaster franchises being just one of
them. But as his work in this position continued, Lorne was
becoming increasingly wearied by the extensive travel.
Wanting to settle down, he was looking for an opportunity to
buy his own business.

Bob Knapp, whose office was in Denver, was the distributor for the state of Colorado. He knew Lorne, but their business relationship was strained because Bob was simply not interested in doing business with Pro-Chem. But when Lorne made the decision to purchase a franchise, he had to go to Bob Knapp. Bob told Lorne about a franchise in Colorado Springs that was available, and they agreed to meet to discuss it.

"When I finished with that first meeting with Lorne," Bob remembered, "he and I had had several serious arguments. After he left I went upstairs to my wife, Claire, and said, 'We have to pray that this guy doesn't buy a franchise. He's going to be nothing but trouble.'"

In spite of his difficulty with Bob, Lorne decided to bid on the business. Although there were two other men in the bidding, the owner decided to sell to Lorne. The very morning that Lorne found out that his bid had been accepted, he also discovered that he had lost his job with Pro-Chem. His career with the ServiceMaster family was now indelibly determined.

WHAT MAKES YOU TICK?

As Lorne's distributor, Bob had occasion to meet with Lorne frequently. Throughout the course of their relationship, and in spite of the fact that Lorne didn't buy ServiceMaster chemicals and several times had a struggle paying his fees, Bob consistently sought to serve him.

"We had constant tension," Bob said. "For instance, Lorne would come to training meetings and always be argumentative and somewhat of an obstacle." Still, Bob believed that it was his responsibility to give of himself to Lorne.

One day Lorne called Bob's wife, Claire, and said, "I have got to know what makes Bob tick." Then he began to list his own failings. "I don't buy the chemicals, I always give Bob trouble, but still he doesn't treat me any differently than he does anybody else. He gives me everything I need and works to build my loyalty in other ways."

As a result of Bob's consistent service to Lorne, a very special relationship gradually developed. Lorne and Bob began to meet weekly in Castle Rock, a city about halfway between Denver and Colorado Springs, for a Bible study. "I prayed to accept Jesus Christ as my Savior," Lorne recalled, "in a J. C. Penney parking lot. When Bob and Claire prayed that I wouldn't buy the business, they were praying for something that wasn't the Lord's will. All along it was the Lord's plan to use them in my life."

At first Lorne's wife Terri was resistant to his Christianity, stating that she wasn't interested in being one of "those hypocrites." "If it does something in Lorne's life," she declared, "I will consider it." Within a year after Lorne's conversion, his wife, Terri became a Christian.

Lorne and Terri think of Bob and Claire as a second set of parents and see their influence as instrumental in the success of their marriage.

"Lorne might say that we are like father and son," echoed Bob, "but I think we are more like brothers. We talk openly about our problems. And now as I look at Lorne in his present position, he is perhaps the greatest single trophy that anyone would want. These relationships are what this business is all about…not the financial pay off, not the fees." In October 1991 Lorne Dillon sold his business and joined the family at the ServiceMaster Clean home office. He is presently serving as the vice president of franchise markets.

If They Give an Invitation, I'm Going Forward

The early 1970s were a pivotal time in Bob and Claire Knapp's lives. They went to a church that was adjacent to Wheaton College, where Bob had earned a degree in physics. Bob had heard about ServiceMaster from his friends Ken Hansen, Dick Armstrong, and Alan Moore, who also attended the church with him.

Bob's choice of a major, physics, although unusual, has served him well. "I've never used the physics a day in my life," he admitted. "But from it I gained a valuable education. It taught me about the decision-making process. It has been a great asset to me in my business career, as it taught me how to analyze variables and choose the one that is going to be the most productive." After college, Bob went into the army with a commission and spent two years in the Signal Corps. He held a position with Teletype Corporation before and after his military service, and then he went back to school, pursuing a master's degree in Business Administration.

"My dad owned his own industrial design firm and, as part of my course work, I did a study of his business. Interestingly, I ended up suggesting that he should sell his business, which he did." During the five years that they worked together, Bob learned a lot from his father's experiences. "As I worked with my dad, I was able to observe the tension between risk and reward. I was able to identify my own interests and become accountable or responsible for the decisions I made. As I watched my dad make decisions that were sometimes anguishing, I became acquainted with the frustration of failure and the joy of success."

Bob then spent one more year trying to help a friend who was going out of business and by 1972, the stage was fully set for his involvement in ServiceMaster.

"I was unemployed, and it was ServiceMaster's twenty-fifth anniversary. I was invited by my friends from church to attend the annual shareholders meeting, which was being held at Downers Grove. Marion E. Wade opened the meeting with an overview of the company. His enthusiasm was infectious. Ken Hansen spoke next on the state of the company. In 1972 the country was in a recession, and the speakers pointed out that the cleaning business was essentially a recession-proof industry. They recognized that even though some optional work might be lost, 'dirt isn't going to disappear just because the economy is bad.' The meeting was held in a tent, on ServiceMaster's home office property, and sawdust covered the ground. It reminded me of an old revival tent meeting. I remember telling Claire, half in earnest, 'If this man gives an invitation, I am going forward.'"

ANSWERING THE CALL

Bob was interviewed and hired by Ed Morgan, who told him that he would be in training for six to ten months while they decided where to assign him. One week into the training, Ed called Bob and said, "We are going to accelerate your training a bit." Two or three weeks after that Bob and his wife were sent to Denver, where Dick Armstrong gave him a week of training before he became the manager of the branch office there. "Honestly," Bob confessed, "at that time I hardly knew what a 'roto' was."

Bob stayed in that position for a year and a half before he was promoted to the position of regional manager. In January 1975 he was made the manager of the Franchise West Division, and in January of 1976 he was promoted to the position of vice president of Residential and Commercial Services (ResCom), the predecessor to ServiceMaster Clean, where he served until August 1979.

As vice president, one of Bob's responsibilities was to sell off the branch offices that the company owned at the time. He was curious, however, to see whether or not a pure distributorship business would work. "I was concerned because I saw the tension that was created when a distributor owned his own franchise. If these owner/distributors would get a big fire job they would be too busy to go visit the franchisee."

As it turned out, the last distributorship left to sell was in Denver. It was an area that was hard to market because, although the territory was most of the state of Colorado, it wasn't producing much revenue. Claire and Bob loved Denver and decided that they should take the business themselves, even though it meant that he would have to take a 70 percent cut in pay. As Bob thought over his business plan, he could foresee that in 30 months he would be able to build the business to the point where he would again achieve his former income levels.

"That was a rather large entrepreneurial risk," Bob admitted. "But with the support of the family and God's help, it worked. I had had the unique opportunity to spend three or four years going around the country seeing good and bad decisions that distributors made. I knew I could build a model for the business that would capitalize on all the strengths of ServiceMaster and my own experience."

EFFECTIVE STEWARDSHIP

From the beginning of his relationship with the ServiceMaster family, Bob has valued the four corporate objectives. "As a personal lifestyle I buy them entirely. I also saw my distributorship as an opportunity to work not only with people's businesses, but with the whole person. Claire and I positioned ourselves to be more than mere business counselors. We wanted to help our franchisees in other areas of their lives. We knew that if we helped them be successful in their personal lives, their businesses would be successful, too."

As Bob superintended the franchises in his group, he used the principles found in a book about parenting. *The Effective Father*,[2] by Gordon MacDonald, was an important book for Bob, not only in the parenting of his two daughters, but also in the building of his business relationships. He took the six principles presented in the book and molded them to fit his role as a distributor. He saw how he could effectively nurture others in his business in the same way that he had been nurtured by those in the ServiceMaster home office. He then presented the principles to franchisees who were also employers.

The first principle: If I am an effective employer it is because I have deliberately set out as one of my life's highest priorities the creation of conditions in my business that will stimulate my employees to grow to their full human potential.

Bob remembers Ken Hansen as a person who loved to develop people. He was an encourager and wanted to see people grow. For instance, on one occasion when Bob had to give a presentation to the ServiceMaster board, Ken called him into his office and told him to rehearse the speech right there in front of him. When Bob was finished, Ken counseled him to watch his "split infinitives." Bob admits that he had to go back to his secretary's office and ask what a split infinitive was. "That was the kind of person Ken Hansen was—he helped those around him to be the best that they could be."

When Bob decided to leave the home office and buy a distributorship, it was Ken who asked him the number of people he thought he would be able to minister to in the new position. Once he was satisfied with Bob's answer, Ken stood and put his arms around him. "I will pray for you," he promised.

"Once every six months for as long as he lived Ken would call me very early in the morning and ask, 'How are things going? What can I pray for?' That was an incredible encouragement. I was never in his presence without learning something. He was an incredible mentor."

Bob defines success as taking the gifts that God has given him and others around him and developing them. He continually encourages, prays for, and creates environments in which men like Lorne Dillon and Andy Beal—who have since joined the home office staff also—could prosper.

The second principle: If I am going to be an effective employer it is because I have devoted myself to become an instrument and model of human experience to my employees.

"I wanted to earn the right to share with the franchise owners in other areas of their lives," Bob stated compassionately. "The only way I could do this for them was to assure them that they were going to get 110 percent out of me. Once they learned that they were going to be treated in a way beyond what was required in our contracts, I felt I had the right to invade other areas of their life. The application of the corporate objectives allowed me to speak to all of the areas of their lives. Serving as a developer of people was one of my strong suits."

The third principle: If I am an effective employer it is because I have sharpened my sensitivity to my employees' needs, committed my inner being to God's laws, and fixed a foresightful eye on opportunities and hazards ahead. I want to make sure that every business experience builds my employees up and matures them.

From the very beginning Bob took to heart God's counsel to Joshua: "Be strong and very courageous; be careful to do according to all the law [upon which] you shall meditate day and night…for then you will make your way prosperous, and then you will have success" (Joshua 1:7-8, NASB).

Ken Wessner saw this heart in Bob before he left the corporate offices. " Bob," Ken told him, "one of your problems is that you have the heart of a pastor." Bob knew that Ken was implying that he needed to be a general, rather than a pastor, if he was going to lead an organization. Bob's heart, however, was to help others with the details of life. In his position with the home office, he felt more like an evangelist. He never got to see those he was training become successful. He'd never had the joy of watching transformation in another person's life. "That was and is my heart. That is where I am strongest," Bob declared. "If you are dealing with an individual, you have to consider dealing with the whole person so that his success isn't compartmentalized in just one area of his life, such as his business. You have to think of all aspects of his life."

The fourth principle: If I am an effective employer it is because I am filling my employee's lives with perspectives and patterns which produce wisdom; I am lovingly purging their lives of unwholesome influences and tendencies that impede their progress toward maturity.

This personal and intense involvement in lives was something that had been modeled for Bob by Ken Wessner. Bob remembered one instance when Ken Wessner unblushingly told him that he had failed in meeting his goals, even though Bob's numbers were significantly better than the national franchise norms. "He knew what we were capable of producing and wouldn't let us get by with less than that."

Once as Bob reflected on Ken's attitudes and actions, he went to his office. "'Wes, is it fair to say that when I come through your office door you see a chunk of coal, and in the corner of that chunk is a little glistening bit that could possibly be a diamond, and that you are going to beat the stuffing out of it to see just how big that diamond is?' That was the gift that Ken Wessner had. He was never satisfied with 'adequate.' He had a way of making very uncomfortable statements, and he was hard on me personally, but I valued that tremendously. He was honing my character, and I count him, next to my father, as one of the most influential people in shaping my life."

The fifth principle: If I am an effective employer it is because I accept and affirm my employees for who they are, appreciate them for what they are accomplishing, and cover them with affection because they are mine.

"All of our people really felt that they were part of a family. They knew they were safe and that they would be treated fairly. If I needed to correct them, I would do it out of love for them. They knew where our loyalties were, and they were loyal to us in return. They were much more teachable because of the depth of our relationships. I always tried to focus on the potential of the individual and not merely on the action committed."

The sixth principle: If I am an effective employer it is because I am aware that I always live on the edge of ineffectiveness and must continually reach out to God for wisdom and skill to accomplish my task.

Bob has continually looked to God for wisdom and skill. Although he's been exceedingly effective, both as a father and as a businessman, he doesn't take the credit for himself. He lives by a Bible passage in the book of Deuteronomy that teaches him that the blessings he's realized are all from God's hand. When he sold his distributorship back to ServiceMaster in 1996, it had 57 franchises producing considerable annual revenues.

Bob's success isn't limited to his material wealth, however. Both of his daughters and their husbands are missionaries, following in their father's faith—one serving in Mongolia and the other in Spain. In addition, he is the chairman of the board of *Women of the Harvest*, a group that supports and encourages women in cross-cultural missions work, as well as other Christian charitable concerns. Bob is also busy helping ServiceMaster Clean franchisees with their business and personal financial planning.

In 1982, Bob and Claire Knapp received the Marion E. Wade Master Award. That they attained the highest level of achievement in ServiceMaster is just a reflection of the manner in which they have lived as servants—or shepherds, if you will—to those whom God has placed in their care. They've embodied the very essence of ServiceMaster's corporate objectives, and their legacy will live on, even through their retirement, in the lives of the people they have effectively fathered.

A SEEMINGLY INSIGNIFICANT SERVICE

The Story of Bob and Becky Smith

"We must become servants, servants first of all of the Lord and then, in His name, servants unto all."

Marion E. Wade[1]

When Dora, a dear 84-year-old lady, looked over the damage at her home, she was devastated. All of her memories, her precious belongings, were either ruined or damaged. As hard as it was for her to deal with the realities of two-thirds of her home being damaged by fire, the blow that she received the following day was even worse: her beloved husband was diagnosed with colon cancer. Needless to say, Dora was overwhelmed and crushed. It seemed to her that her entire life had burned down around her. The physicians outlined for her and her husband the surgery, chemotherapy, and radiation treatments that were to come.

Such a situation tests the strongest of people under even the best of circumstances, but Dora and her husband were facing it without the comfort of their home, their belongings, their memories.

As Faye and Ruth, fire restoration specialists, assessed the damage to Dora's home and saw the trauma that she had undergone and had yet to face, they went into action. They knew that they were called to do something more for this sweet lady and her husband. So with great compassion and care, they stepped into her life. They moved Dora and her husband into an apartment and rush-cleaned the basic necessities so that Dora and her husband could settle in before his surgery.

Faye and Ruth helped Dora shop for new furniture for her dining room. On their own, they purchased lampshades, curtains, and other household items so that Dora wouldn't be forced to leave her husband during this crucial time. They worked diligently to restore Dora's precious memories: her photo albums were restored; pictures and picture frames were bought and reset; the family Bible was redone, as well as other special mementos. Faye and Ruth did these things without being asked. They wanted to be sure that when Dora was finally able to return home, it would seem like home again.

Faye, the fire restoration manager, and Ruth, her assistant, are both extremely busy women. But because they have been taught to see their job as a service, they knew they had to go the extra mile so that Dora would be free to care for her husband. Tammy, a crew leader, spent time consoling Dora and reminding her of God's faithfulness even in the midst of this terrible trial.

Bob and Becky Smith, owners of ServiceMaster of St. Charles, Clayton, and Westport in St. Peters, Missouri, know that their competitors do what is required by insurance companies. But they believe that their business has a higher calling. They believe that they must "go beyond what is expected to accommodate the unique needs of our customers. It's the small things that you can do for people that makes all the difference."

MR. PERSONALITY

Bob Smith's high-school years were spent working in a full-service gas station. As Bob watched Bruce, the owner of the business, deal with his customers, he learned a valuable lesson: "The customer is always right."

"I always liked my boss because he was 'Mr. Personality.' As an employee, I saw the way that some customers tried to take advantage of him. I could see that they were wrong, and as I look back on it, my boss probably knew that too. I would think, *that guy has no right to ask for that!* But Bruce taught me, 'The customer is always right'—even when it was obvious that he was wrong. He taught me that if the customer felt like he had won in any given situation, he'd come back, and he'd refer his friends back, too. I've always tried to make Bruce's philosophy my own, knowing that if I did, I would be successful. I always wanted to own my own business, and thanks to Bruce, I had a credo to guide me."

AN UNAPOLOGETIC EMPHASIS

After graduating from high school, Bob went on to Taylor University, where he majored in Business Administration. It was there in 1977, as a senior, that he was first formally introduced to ServiceMaster. As the ServiceMaster representative spent time with the class, Bob knew that this was a company he could work with.

"I found their unapologetic emphasis on integrity and faith, and their strong moral commitment of honoring God, especially attractive. I saw how my personal faith dovetailed with their corporate objectives and goals. It certainly wasn't what I expected from the corporate world," Bob admitted. "There was no apology for their faith, while there was also no demand that anyone had to believe the way they did. It was clear, though, that they were very comfortable with proclaiming their position."

Bob joined the ServiceMaster hospital division upon graduation and, after a time of further training, found himself managing housekeepers. Bob loved the honesty and integrity that was displayed daily at the company. He also relished the enormous growth, high energy, and quick advancement potential. He remembers this as a time of great excitement.

Bob became the director of housekeeping for St. Louis University Hospital after three years and stayed with the hospital division for a total of eight years. Since the workers in the hospital were direct employees of ServiceMaster, Bob was responsible for all the human resource problems, paperwork, payroll, time sheets, and paychecks, in addition to providing the normal assistance to the hospital. "We were, in effect, running our own business there. I was responsible for that profit center, but since we had all the payroll, hiring, firing, and benefit concerns too, it was like running my own business."

No Set Limits

All through his years of work, Bob had always been drawn to people who went into business for themselves. As a leader in the hospital division, Bob was invited to attend a ServiceMaster award conference in Palm Beach, Florida. It was there, while associating with highly successful franchisees and men from Management Services, that Bob began to see the potential available in ownership.

"I was very intrigued by what the franchisees had to say. I heard about the size of the businesses that they were operating and the financial rewards available. After that meeting, I was excited about the possibilities of business ownership. In the hospital division I felt like I had a lot on the ball and that I could offer the company my dedication. I discovered that these franchise owners felt the same way. But I also learned that if I owned my own business, no one would set limits on what I could earn, except myself."

Bob and Henry Citchen, a friend from ServiceMaster's hospital division, joined forces in the early 1980s. While Bob retained his position with ServiceMaster, Henry sought to build the business. Although it was a full six months before they landed their first commercial account, a property management company, Bob and Henry were committed to soliciting only large accounts. "We didn't start out small," Bob remembered. "The kind of buildings we wanted to go after were the big ones. When you don't have any other business, though, it's hard to convince people that you can do the job. But we finally convinced one fellow, and we held onto that account for 15 years. Our objective from the start was to pursue larger accounts that we could staff with a supervisor and several employees. That way we could go to one location and build more revenue."

During these early years, Bob helped in putting together the proposals and job estimates. Henry tried to set up appointments late in the afternoon so that Bob could make it to the presentations after work. In addition, Bob frequently helped out in the actual production of the work.

"Since most of the cleaning was done in the evenings, I would go over and help if I was in town. I would strip floors and clean carpets. Early on my involvement was limited because I wasn't involved in the day-to-day operations. In 1984 I made the decision that it was time to leave my position with ServiceMaster and go into the commercial services business full time." Bob's wife, Becky, was also a business major who specialized in accounting, so she joined the business and has been in charge of the books ever since.

In 1990, Bob purchased Henry's shares in the endeavor and subsequently has built an excellent business in both commercial services and disaster restoration. ServiceMaster Contract Services (Bob's commercial services division) employs 200 while his disaster restoration business,

ServiceMaster of St. Charles, Clayton, and Westport, employs 25. Together their annual revenues are in the top twenty in the ServiceMaster Clean family. In 1997, Bob and Becky won the Marion E. Wade Master Award for excellence, growth, and stability.

One Crucial Difference

Accommodating is the motto that Bob has chosen for his business. "From the very beginning we have sought to be a 'can-do' company. We wanted to ensure that if our customers were going to talk about us, they would say that we do whatever they ask us to." Bob has instructed all his employees to follow through on this philosophy, even if it means that they are doing extra work.

"If a customer asks our workers to do something out of the ordinary, then they're taught to go ahead and serve them. They report the extra work to their supervisor, who then contacts the customer to see if this is something they want to add to their regular cleaning schedule. If something comes up, such as an unexpected visit from an important person, and our customers need extra work done, we do everything we can to accommodate them. We'll try to jump through any hoop so that we can make them look good. We can't forget that we're a *service* business. Anybody can run a cleaning company, and there is a great difference between that and being in *service*."

Selling the Company to the Employee

Bob understands that one of the biggest obstacles facing his business today is finding and keeping the right kind of personnel. In these times of nearly nonexistent unemployment, Bob has had to think of innovative ways to surround himself with the kind of employees that will continue to make the company successful.

"We have had to work harder at training and developing our people. We've tried to make the company attractive to our employees. We keep our commitments to them: commitments to provide them with uniforms, training, and financial compensation. We have to sell our company to our employees as well as our customers. We've had to give holiday, vacation, and even sick pay to our tenured part-time employees. We give bonuses to people who refer friends or family to us. We give service pins and recognize employees in front of their peers for longevity. We have a quarterly newsletter acknowledging all the new team members and those who have gotten promotions. If any of them have children in college, we put together care packages in September and in the spring, and we send them out to their kids. We stock the package with post-it pads, pencils, little paper gifts, snacks, and other things like that. We also include a little note that says, 'Your mom or dad works for us, and we want you to work hard. They are very proud of you and they're glad that you're pursuing higher education.'"

Although two of Bob and Becky's three girls are in college, that doesn't mean that they're exempt from working in the business when they're home from school. For instance, this last Christmas a hotel had a major pipe break from freezing temperatures. It flooded the lobby and many of the rooms. So at 11:00 p.m., Bob mobilized Becky and their three girls, Nicky, Tracy, and Cassie, and off they went with "dear old dad." All three daughters have learned the importance of being there for the customer, no matter how inconvenient that might be.

SERVANT-LEADERS

In all of his relationships, whether with employees or customers, Bob is concerned about the way that his life impacts those around him. "Does my life reflect Christ?" he wonders. "Do I live out the corporate objectives? Forgive the cliche," he said, "but does my walk match my talk? I believe that our highest priority is to be servant-leaders."

For Bob, servant-leadership means investing time in the lives of others. "If you take the corporate objectives to heart, if you live them out, it means that you'll not only be blessed, but you will also be successful. That will happen because success and blessing will be measured in how you've helped others develop."

"We believe that our customers and our employees—indeed, all of our resources—are blessings from God. He has blessed us with the people in this business, and we need to commit ourselves to developing those relationships. We've tried to build these relationships on a foundation of honesty, respect, fairness, tenderness, and a deep concern for helping others succeed."

CORPORATE OBJECTIVES PLAYED OUT IN LOVING ARMS

Fred Citchen, Bob's operations manager for the last 18 years, has learned how important the corporate objectives really are. On one occasion he was called on to provide a ride to work for one of the employees, Larome, or "Peppy," as he is better known. When Fred arrived to pick up Peppy, Peppy asked Fred to wait until one of his children was safely off the school bus. As Fred waited, he became impatient and thought, *This waiting is going to make me late arriving at the job site.* Finally the school bus arrived, and Peppy went to the bus and picked up his little ten-year-old stepson. The boy was badly deformed, a paraplegic. When Fred saw the compassion that Peppy had for this child and how the child hugged his neck, he asked God to forgive him for his impatience. "Here I was thinking that Peppy was going to make me late to my job," Fred admitted, "and then I realized what life was really about: commitment to family, friends, and our relationship to Christ." To this day, Peppy remains a loyal and dependable employee, serving the same account for the past 15 years. "He really exemplifies what Christ wants us to be: faithful, committed, and caring to all those He puts us in contact with."

Bob and Becky Smith are people who believe wholeheartedly that they are servants. Whether they're faced with unexpected demands from a client or any unusual needs of their employees, their ServiceMaster business is merely a platform from which they seek to accommodate those around them and model servant-leadership.

TEACHING IS YOUR BUSINESS

The Story of Ian England

*"Learning should be the business of the firm,
and the opportunities provided should expand
beyond areas directly related to business."*
C. William Pollard[1]

After graduating from high school, Ian England began his education in his life's vocation with ServiceMaster as a commercial crew chief in 1976. After a few years as a carpet cleaner, he purchased a commercial franchise, and in 1978 he went out on his own, overseeing a small territory in the city of Toronto.

Although Ian was a skilled technician, he hadn't yet learned the lessons that he needed to learn. His foray into the world of entrepreneurship was short-lived; in six months the business failed. "It was a disaster," Ian remembers. But Ian wasn't finished with ServiceMaster, and the lessons that he learned in his first experience on his own were pivotal in shaping him as a teacher. It was there, in the school of hard knocks, that Ian learned the humility and tenacity that have made him the person he is today.

After his business failed, Ian returned to his previous employment as a crew chief and experienced the humiliation of having to admit failure. After several years in this position, he went to work as a salesman and service representative for Thane McNeil, who owned a large franchise in Ontario. In ServiceMaster Thane's name is almost legendary, as was his impact on people like Ian. Thane graciously chronicled his history with the ServiceMaster family for this book, and what follows is a distillation of his own words:

During the summer of 1953, I was living on Prince Edward Island located in eastern Canada. My father had suffered an untimely death at the age of 63, and I took on the responsibility of supporting my mother and younger sisters. Even though I had a very marginal education, I continually tried to provide for the family. I worked as a farm hand, sold farm equipment, ran a service station, and butchered. I struggled to survive, and the future didn't seem very promising.

Frank Flack, a man who was dating my sister, came to P.E.I. from Toronto for a vacation. Frank had just invested in a ServiceMaster franchise in Toronto, and he talked with me about the opportunities available in this new company. A few weeks later, I had the privilege of meeting Marion E. Wade and his wife Lillian. Mr. Wade said to me, "You provide the man, and I'll provide a future."

A short time later, Mr. Wade sent me a one-way train ticket to Chicago, and I began a six-month training program with the company. I will always be thankful to God for allowing me to know Marion Wade, a man who's had such a great impact on so many people's lives. I'm also thankful that he lived to see his dream become a reality. He was a man of God and a great humanitarian.

As a young man with a limited education, Marion Wade was struggling just to support his family in Chicago. After a serious accident, Mr. Wade prayed, "Lord, send me people who will help me build a business that will honor You in the marketplace." This prayer demonstrates the uniqueness of Marion Wade. Most men would have been thinking about how they could establish a future for themselves. Instead, he was dreaming about building an organization that would provide an opportunity where many people could own their own businesses while honoring God.

Marion Wade understood that in order for his dream to become a reality, he would have to surround himself with people who shared his vision. He met and recruited to his team Ken Hansen, an ordained minister. As the business began to grow, he continued to surround himself with others who had the same goals. ServiceMaster has become the outstanding organization that it is today because of the men who united with Mr. Wade during those early years.

When I joined ServiceMaster, the entire corporation was producing a gross volume of business of approximately $250,000. Although the company was just beginning, the four corporate objectives were already being practiced, even though they hadn't been officially adopted as the company standard.

Mr. Wade spent many hours with me sharing his vision for the future. He wanted me to see how I could be a part of that vision. I came to realize that we had a lot in common, and he became my mentor, a second father. He made me feel very much a part of the Wade family.

ServiceMaster has been a way of life for me and my family for nearly 50 years. It has allowed me to live out Mr. Wade's dream of business ownership. ServiceMaster wasn't merely a job or even a prosperous investment, it has been a way of life.

One of my greatest joys has been watching people I helped place in business grow successful, while becoming better human beings. It was particularly rewarding for me to have assisted in developing the Spotlight Carpet Cleaning Program in the 1980's. This concept has revolutionized the commercial carpet cleaning industry. Our distributorship, ServiceMaster of Toronto in Mississauga, Ontario, Canada, also introduced the multiple-license concept, thereby offering many more opportunities for new franchise licensees. We were honored to win the Marion E. Wade Master Award of Excellence in 1972 and again in 1990, especially because we had personal knowledge of Mr. Wade's vision, character, and faith.

I will always be thankful that God allowed me to know Marion E. Wade. He's had a tremendous impact on so many people's lives. I'm thankful that he lived to see his ServiceMaster dream become a reality and that I have had a part in that reality.

Thane MacNeill embodies the philosophy of helping people develop that he so appreciated in Marion Wade. The impact of this philosophy was experienced firsthand by men like Ian England.

Between all the lessons that Ian learned from Thane and the failure of his own business, Ian felt he was prepared to venture out on his own again. In 1983 he purchased a franchise in the downtown portion of Toronto and over the next 12 years he built it into the largest commercial franchise in North America at that time. He started with just four employees, but when he sold his business in 1995 he had 11 trucks and 18 employees. Ian decided his next step was to join ServiceMaster's home office staff for he knew that he had something to offer to other franchisees.

Joining with the home office gave Ian the platform to expand his teaching from a small group of close associates to franchisees from around the nation and the world. In his position as vice president for operations in Canada, Ian oversees 156 ServiceMaster Clean franchises, as well as 200 Merry Maids, Furniture Medic, and AmeriSpec franchises.

CALLED TO TEACH

Although Ian's job description may not read "Teacher," that's what Ian loves to do. He loves teaching people how to solve the problems in their businesses. He delights in training them in proper perspectives on relationships with customers and employees—not a slave/master relationship, but rather a partnership. He loves showing them the way to build equity in their businesses so that they can sell them when they want to retire. "Building your own business is different from working all your life for someone else," Ian asserted. "Perhaps you're able to build equity in your home while you work. But this way you work and build equity in your business so that you can sell it off when you want to retire or change jobs."

TEACHING OTHERS TO WIN AS A TEAM

Ian sees the value in working with others and establishing relationships that are mutually beneficial. "It has never been about money for me," he mused. "The largest motivator for me is not what *I can win*, it is what *we can win*. Although I take pride in what I do, I want to win as a team." Ian plays hockey two or three times a week because he loves the comradery of being with others, pursuing a common goal, and achieving it.

"I want to win as a team, not as an individual. For me, it is just not fulfilling as an individual. It is the companionship that we have together where all the fun is." Ian teaches this kind of team spirit when he works with his franchisees, teaching them to find the pleasure in being part of another's success and working with others who are like-minded.

Understanding Marketing

Ian also teaches the franchisees in his area to be tenacious in their marketing. "I learned about marketing from Stan Hunt, a man who started out as a Fuller Brush salesman and then came into ServiceMaster at the age of 50. Stan mentored me and told me that the way to be successful as a marketer was simple: Just work hard and sell, sell, sell."

But Ian recognizes that today the environment for marketing is different. ServiceMaster Clean franchisees don't usually go door to door trying to contact the "housewife" and sell her on the idea of a new scrub brush. "With the development of the dotcoms there is just too much choice," he stated insightfully. "At one time it might have been difficult to research and obtain exactly the kind of service you wanted, but now the market is flooded with hundreds of choices. Who is going to win that race?" he asked. "The person who has the brand name." It's because of this new level of competition that Ian believes that the ServiceMaster Clean brand is so vital. "The yellow vans with the ServiceMaster Clean logo will give the franchisees the winning edge" in an age of over-marketization. "Marketing is also different now because we have to think about globalization. We have to grow and garner the best business practices from around the world and then incorporate them into our business." The world is smaller, and the advantage is to the consumer and the company that can evaluate the changes and grow with them.

A Historical Perspective on Marketing

Ian looks at ServiceMaster Clean's marketing prospects in a very unique way. "In sales," he intoned, "'no' only means 'no' now. It doesn't mean 'no' forever. At ServiceMaster Clean we like to think that we're like the Roman army: nice, shining, marching in columns, and conquering all of Europe. But the truth is that we are more like the Mongol Horde."

Ian instructs his franchisees that they are like the followers of Genghis Khan, who in 1206 swept out of the steppes of Asia in an apocalyptic wave and conquered two-thirds of the known world. "We just sweep over the hills and wipe everybody out," he explained. "I know that doesn't sound very 'sales-ey', but it is the truth. We just don't stop." As he's examined the history of Khan and his followers, he's discovered that they were really very organized. "They weren't just a bunch of guys on horseback." Khan was a supreme military strategist and a clever politician, and his followers were an unstoppable force.

"The truth about the ServiceMaster Clean family is that we are tenacious, and we know what we believe in. We don't stop, we just keep going, running over all our competition. That is a good picture of what we are. Our 3,000+ franchisees are a powerful force sweeping across the land."

In thinking about ServiceMaster Clean's marketing presence, he sees its ultimate triumph. He believes people who have yet to become customers are simply going to be overwhelmed. "There are so many of us, they can't say 'no.' We teach our salespeople to say that our prospective consumers are going to say 'yes' sooner or later. Maybe not today, or next year, but we are going to get them. That's because we actually believe that our service has value. We have an intense and unrelenting belief in the value of our product."

TECHNOLOGY 101

Part of Ian's vision encompasses the developing technologies. "With the development of the Internet we've got to learn how to take hold of technology and use it for our advantage, particularly in the area of training." Although regional and national conferences are beneficial, he recognizes that only a small fraction of businesses are actually affected through them. "That's not enough," Ian stated emphatically. "We're going to have to find a better way to affect people and to train them. We're going to have to find a way to broadcast training into every franchisee's business. The courses that are coming out of the home offices now about fabric care and mold mitigation have to be made available to every business. The technology is there; we have to capture the advantage that we already have. Because we're a big business, we have an opportunity to win the training challenge using technology."

TEACHING PEOPLE HOW TO PUT THEIR LIVES TOGETHER

Ian's burden to teach franchisees isn't limited to technology and marketing, however. He also wants to be part of training people in their life skills, character, and responsible living.

"I didn't come from the poor side of town," he admitted. "But as a franchisee, I got to hire and train people who did. Many of them were lost and directionless when I had the opportunity to meet them and see their lives change for the better."

Ian recalls one particular employee in his business who was an example of this. "This chap had lost his license and hadn't filed his income tax in seven or eight years. We made the decision to take him on, and the first order of business was for him to get his driver's license," Ian recalled. "In order to do that, we had to advance him the money to pay off his fines. Although that was a positive step in the right direction, it wasn't long before the government found him and fined him because of his delinquent taxes. He was pretty discouraged and was beginning to wonder if he would ever be able to win. So we met with the tax people on his behalf and worked out a payment plan. That was in 1985, and he's still with the company today. He just didn't know how to put the pieces together."

EDUCATION IN ETHICS

Ian has had enough business experience to know that sometimes it hurts to be honest. "The business world's acceptable ethic is that a certain level of lying and cheating is okay. The ethical business owner is challenged constantly. It's so easy to think, 'I could do this, and no one would catch me.' It hurts to be honest…especially in the face of competitors who have every intention of cutting corners. It hurts to lose key clients that you have had for years because someone says they will do it cheaper, even though you know in your heart that they can't do it cheaper. They can only do it by cutting corners. In times like that you have to hold the line or lie. Could we do more business?" Ian queried. "Probably. But we don't want to, not at that cost. Most of the people I associate with think the same way too, and that is what we teach. At the end of the day it is not about money. I've been accused of being naive. I am happy that I am."

THE TRUE TENETS OF SUCCESS

From his vantage points both as a successful business owner and as a corporate executive, Ian England has had time to define the meaning of success. For him, the prime way to measure success is by the length of retention of both employees and customers. He admits that early in his career, he defined success by the amount of money he made, which wasn't all bad, since it motivated him to work hard. But, as he achieved his monetary goals, he came to learn that genuine success flows from relationships.

"We have an account that is a large corporation, a nickel mining company in Canada, which we have followed to four different locations," he boasts happily. "We've had their business since 1968; that's some 30-plus years. That is very satisfying."

Ian doesn't think that there is a magic formula for achieving this kind of success. He sees it as a very simple process of being competitive but honest. He believes that accomplishing this kind of success flows out of fulfilling promises and simply doing what you say you are going to do.

Ian's business philosophy is summed up in these words: "Do what you say and don't over-promise on what you can deliver. There is still a lot of room in the world for quality workmanship. After all is said and done, people do understand what quality is, and those are the people who will make great ServiceMaster Clean customers. There are still lots of people who will buy our product because of our quality, and that is the kind of customer we want."

ADVANCED CIVICS

Being the caring teacher that he is, Ian is looking forward to problems that are looming on the horizon. He foresees increasing government intrusion in the small-business world—from health and safety concerns to the way that employees are hired and compensated—as most troubling. Rather than thinking of the government as an enemy, says Ian, ServiceMaster Clean franchises will need to see this as an opportunity—an opportunity to make the government their partner and make the most of that relationship.

"Whether we like it or not," he stated, "they are the silent partner in everything we do.

"We can fight them all we want but they are still going to be our partner. Instead of fighting against this, let's try to find a way to maximize it and make it work for us. Only the big companies are going to be able to figure out the government paperwork. Who can be an expert in health and safety, privacy laws, pay equity laws, and chemical handling laws and disposal? Who could be an expert in all that? Not any one individual. Our small independent competitors won't be able to. For us to succeed we are going to have to embrace our advantage and make it a positive."

I'LL NEVER, NEVER BE A SALESMAN

Even though Ian England's job description is to drive revenue and enforce contracts, he does much more than that. At heart he is a teacher. Whether it's Advanced Civics or Technology 101, Ian brings to his position a heart of intensity, integrity, and commitment to the ServiceMaster Clean ideals.

As a child Ian observed his father's career in sales and knew it wasn't for him. He confessed, "I hated sales and swore that I would never be a salesman. I was never going to be in sales — never. The truth is that I wanted to teach." Although he's presently vice president of operations, Ian England is really a teacher, and he's living out vital lessons in ethical, practical, and tenacious business practices for all the franchisees who have the privilege to hear and learn from him.

AN AFFAIR
OF THE HEART

The Story of Bob and Dee McDonell

"...*your job becomes more than a job. It
becomes a calling. It is the ministry by which
you glorify God...who is your silent Partner.*"

Marion E. Wade[1]

Bob McDonell is a man with a heart. In talking with
him, it doesn't take long to discover that his heart
is clearly and irrevocably centered on his faith in God. Mild-
mannered and soft-spoken, never lacking a smile, Bob's focus
has never wavered from the core values that have informed
and motivated him through the years. He is today what he
was some 20-plus years ago, a family man, a man of faith.

Even now, at a time when he could be relaxing and rest-
ing on his laurels, Bob and his wife, Brenda, still sense God's
call to extend a helping hand to others. For instance, often on
Sunday afternoons they entertain Hispanic families in their

home; these are families without fathers, families that need encouragement and a helping hand. His wife, Brenda, holds Bible clubs for children in their front yard. Honoring God in all he does is much more to Bob than a slogan on a wall—it's the essence and reason of his being. His relationship, first with God, and secondarily with his family at home and in ServiceMaster, is a current that's run deeply through Bob. For Bob, it's an affair of his heart.

"Mac," as his friends call him, (and who isn't his friend?) is a man who's known both joys and heartaches. He's walked through several career changes, great successes as a franchisee and a distributor, and numberless clouded days, as the sun was temporarily blotted out by events that can never be prepared for. Though his heart's been crushed, it's never wavered from his center.

"AND THE WINNER IS..."

These days you'll find Mac touting the latest products and equipment. He's the director of products and vendor relations for ServiceMaster Clean in Memphis, Tennessee. This is a position that places him in direct contact with the franchisees, and the vendors and manufacturers of the products and equipment that they use. At every ServiceMaster Clean convention, Mac is the one person that *everyone* wants to hear from. That's because he's the man who's in charge of giving away all those wonderful prizes. He develops and maintains relationships with the companies that sell to the franchisees, and he's the one who oversees the setting up of those interesting displays at the Expo center. But Mac hasn't always been a part of ServiceMaster's home office; in fact, his link to the ServiceMaster family began very differently— almost a lifetime ago—in Wheaton, Illinois.

THE WHEATON CONNECTION

Wheaton College is a private, interdenominational Christian college that was established in Wheaton, Illinois, in

1860. Its graduates include such luminaries as Billy Graham, but Wheaton College has another claim to fame—it's what is known as the ServiceMaster connection. In fact, it has even honored ServiceMaster's founder, Marion E. Wade, with a study center named in his honor.

In 1978, Mac and his wife, Dee, were looking to change the direction of their career. Mac was employed by National Gypsum in sales and marketing, and because the building industry was burgeoning, his employer wanted to promote him, but a promotion would necessitate a move. For Mac, uprooting his three children from their schools and neighborhoods was not an option. His relationships with the Wheaton College family were also a consideration. "You can't live in Wheaton, be born there, go to school there, and have a wife that goes to Wheaton College, and not know about ServiceMaster. There's a joke around the company," Bob laughed, "that you can't get a job with ServiceMaster, unless you graduated from Wheaton."

Mac and Dee were also drawn to ServiceMaster because of the character of the people that were a part of the company. He was attracted by the honesty and values that guide those who were in leadership positions, especially Ken Hansen and Ken Wessner. Mac was also attracted by the opportunity he saw to be his own boss, to be the one who determined his own success or failure. As he and his wife considered the options before them, it was the quality of the people and the focus of the business that won them over. Mac realized that although the God-centered values were key issues to the leaders of the company, there was also great business acumen and drive. "We knew that you couldn't have this pie-in-the-sky theory of good works and integrity and honesty without taking care of the shareholders. There had to be a balance. We looked carefully at that, and saw there was balance in the company." So, in the late 1970's Mac and his wife, Dee, opened a contract services business, and three years later they purchased a distributorship.

"We were pretty frugal with our money in those days. We didn't have any debt aside from our home mortgage. That's due in part to Ken Hansen's influence. On one hand, Ken was very generous and compassionate, but on the other hand, he was really fiscally conservative. Ken preached that our customers were the ones who were paying our bills and that we should be very careful with the money. But this wasn't something that he merely preached without living it out himself. Ken traveled a lot," Mac smiled, "but he seldom carried a suitcase. He would just wash his clothes out in the sink, in the hotel, at night. He believed that there was a right way to take care of his assets, whether those assets were a dollar bill or a pair of shorts. All the founders were like that. They were men of character and honesty who weren't looking for the limelight. Does that mean that he went around with a holier-than-thou attitude all the time? No, but it did mean that his value system had something more to it than just the bottom line."

As Mac and Dee put their company together they found that the most difficult obstacle they had to overcome was finding people with discipline and commitment—people who were willing to follow the proven systems to reach their objectives. "For us it wasn't an option. When I quit my job at National Gypsum I had three kids who were going to head off to college. My kids thought that I was nuts, but Dee supported me," Mac remembered. "Franchisees today have to be disciplined if they're going to be successful. They have to follow the systems that the founders set in place, and that others have built on."

As Mac and Dee saw their business grow, they were careful to adhere to the standards they had learned from Ken Hansen. "We were frugal," Mac confessed. "Because of the distributorship we did a lot of driving back and forth in Illinois and Nebraska. Dee was the distributor, and I was the product person. We didn't have a lot of extra money, so when we traveled, we didn't stay in motels. We slept in the van and took sleeping bags with us. We had a little heater that we used so that the products we were transporting wouldn't freeze. We would plug in the heater at Super 8's, and we slept in the vans. These weren't cushy vans; they were cargo vans. We had a one-ton van and would go back and forth every weekend."

FROM SINGLE MOM TO CORPORATE MANAGER

Although Mac and Dee were incredibly frugal with themselves, they were kind and generous with their employees. One employee came into the business as a single mom with three children. Bob and Dee became part of her family, and she has since achieved goals far beyond her dreams. She worked for them for 10 years and then went through ServiceMaster's management training program. She is now among the top regional people in the home office today. She became a Christian because of Mac's witness, and now her life is really on track. "She is a successful woman today because of her relationship with ServiceMaster," Mac boasted.

On many occasions in the early days of his business, Mac found himself in the role of counselor. The questions that Mac and Dee were asked were the kinds of questions that children ask their parents. But to their employees, Mac and Dee weren't just business owners, they were "mom and dad." So the employees would bring all their questions to them, whether financial or familial. Sometimes Mac would silently pray, "Lord, help me…what is the answer here?" There were times when he would be at a loss for words, but he trusted that God would help him. "I think that if we fill that role of mother and father, instead of just business owner, we can train and keep good employees. I think sometimes employees are treated more like chattel property or mere objects of labor. We tried never to do that. We wanted them to feel comfortable with us."

THE FRANCHISE AS FAMILY

Mac's management philosophy is simple: "I believe that everybody wants to do well. Everyone has visions and goals.

I haven't met anyone who gets up in the morning and says, 'I want to be a jerk today.' So, when people do dumb things, having an employer who understands that their mistakes aren't intentional, is important. A good employer also has to become part of the employees' lives. We believed that the business had to be a family, not just a job, if we were going to be successful. In fact," Bob said, "we had people who sought our business out as a place to work. It wasn't because we were paying a lot more than anyone or because we were known as a 'party company.' It was because we had cared for our people. We believed that they were individuals, and all of them were children of God, like us. That is the way that we lived in our business. So, we never had any trouble getting people to work for us. We didn't lose many employees, either."

Sometimes this philosophy of family cost Mac. One woman who had come to work for him had been estranged from her family. She was a "down-and-outer." She had no teeth, was very rough around the edges, and worked part time for him at night for seven years. During the day she would call him for advice or help, or just for human contact. "She would talk and talk. I was busy, and I would desperately want to say, 'I have other things to do,' but I didn't. I tried to make everyone feel a part of the family so that the employees would enjoy coming to work. That is the greatest opportunity that ServiceMaster Clean offers. There is no other company in the world who does what we do for our franchisees, for our employees."

THE IMAGE OF SUCCESS

If you asked Mac what one word would best describe his business' character, he thinks it would be the word, *Image*. "Our people were always uniformed—that was before it was fashionable or became a directive. They were in a real uniform, and we saw to it that the uniform was pressed. Our vehicles were always clean," Mac recalled. "The first thing that the customer sees is image, and you never get a second chance to impress with image. The customer perceives that the business you will conduct in their home will look like what you look like. Image says volumes to a prospective customer. For that reason, we used to give new franchise owners two books: *Dress for Success* by John T. Molloy and *The Effective Father* by Gordon MacDonald. We asked them to read these two books. I would also tell them that I wanted people to see the Lord's image in our businesses as well. Some people would say that you can't really be like this, but we proved that you could."

Mac will know he's been successful if he hears God say to him, "Well done, good and faithful servant." "I have made more money than I ever dreamed possible," Mac acknowledges. "Today I couldn't spend it all. It is meaningless to me. I don't owe a penny to anybody. In the end it will rust—it's really just meaningless. Even the paycheck I get today isn't important. In fact, I don't know what my salary is. It is an automatic deposit. That's because, for me, it really isn't important. I enjoy doing what I do, and I enjoy the people. But most of all I hope that the corporate values live on. Maybe someday I'll just give all the money away. Success isn't financial, it's being able to lead one more person or tell one more person the truth."

Some might say that it's easy for Mac to have faith; after all, he's got everything: a successful career, and a fine family. And although it's true that Bob has prospered, he has also walked through the devastation that only a widower knows.

In 1992, on one of her many trips to visit the family of franchises under their care, Bob's partner and dear wife, Dee, was run off the road by an 18-wheeler and killed. "We were married 33 years," Mac said softly, "and were 100 percent partners. I loved her then, and I still love her now. I will love her forever. She was a tremendous example to everyone who knew her. You know, at one point I realized that I had never in the history of our business written my wife a paycheck.

Not once. We were each working 60, 70, 80 hours a week, and we got just one paycheck. She never complained, and she never mentioned a word about it."

A CHANGE OF CAREER

In 1995, Mac sold his distributorship back to ServiceMaster Clean and went to work for the home office, but his heart has never changed. In his position as the director of products and vendor relations, he still sees his role as that of a counselor, motivator, preacher, and father. Loving and caring for the franchisees is something that Mac continues to work at. "I want them to know and feel that I care for them, without any phony baloney. I believe that if they sense that, their hearts will be happy, and they'll just keep going with their eye on the mark. For Dee and I, it was the integrity and the value of the company that was paramount. I believe in the people in the company, and I believe that our franchisees will stay happy when it is, for them too, an affair of the heart."

In 1996 Mac was blessed to marry Brenda, a widow whose husband had been tragically murdered by a disgruntled employee. "We both miss our spouses. We both feel blessed, though. We had known each other for years because we were both in the same church together and our kids were, too. We really feel that the Lord has blessed us a second time. Although I will always miss my first wife, Brenda and I have been able to make a new life, still missing our old spouses."

Mac and Dee's children are still involved in ServiceMaster. "Our kids are heavily involved carrying on those traditions. They are individuals and adults now, and I'm so glad that they are still with the company; two are franchise owners, and his daughter is a marketer. ServiceMaster kept our family together. Our kids grew up working in the business. Although it's true that they probably felt some of our troubles, they were blessed too. The children had a job when they wanted it, and the business literally paid for all three of them to go through school. I have been really blessed."

Even though Mac may someday retire and possibly pursue other avenues of ministry, his love for God, and his desire to serve people, won't ever retire. During his great successes and his undeniable tragedies, he's kept his eye on the goal and his heart focused on the prize of pleasing God and loving others. For Mac, it's always been an affair of the heart...an affair that will never end.

A TEAM BUILDER

The Story of Randy McCall

> *"This sense of responsibility toward others...*
> *results in a team spirit, which though it can't*
> *guarantee a pennant, at least provides more*
> *of a chance for one."*
>
> Marion E. Wade[1]

If you ever have the opportunity to meet Randy McCall, don't think that his soft-spoken Southern drawl or friendly manner is merely a front. Randy McCall is friendly and caring because he is, at his core, a team-builder. Every aspect of his business is focused on building a team that will provide opportunities for people to grow. His vocation has been concentrated on providing opportunities for others—for his sons first, but equally for his team member-employees as well.

THE HOME TEAM

The late 1950s were years of innocence and lightheartedness for most of the young men growing up near the white sandy beaches, tropical emerald-green water, and moderate climate of Panama City, Florida. Indeed, many of Randy's friends spent their free time fishing or sunbathing on the 27 miles of great beaches. By contrast, Randy was serving hamburgers, hot dogs, drinks, and ice cream to tourists and regulars at his parents' two drive-in restaurants.

"I started working in those businesses when I was 12 or 13 years old. I worked all through high school. I started off working four or five hours a day after school. Pretty soon I was working late with my parents who were there 14-16 hours a day. My dad started his days at 9:00 a.m. and didn't close up until 11:00 at night. As I grew up I spent a lot of hours there, and a lot of nights I even helped close up. I realized pretty quickly that being in business for yourself requires hard work and sacrifice, but I also knew that it was something I wanted to do."

While it might appear to the casual onlooker that Randy's adolescence was wasted in a dead-end job, the soul of a player-manager was being shaped. After high school, Randy went on to Georgia Tech, graduating with a degree in Industrial Management. But before he finished his graduate studies in Business Administration, he decided it was time to join the workforce. Don't think that he hasn't completed his business education, though: "I learned it the hard way, I reckon," he quipped in his quintessential Southern style.

TRIPLE-A TRAINING

From college, Randy went to work for a clothing manufacturer and was responsible, as the regional manager, for overseeing operations in two plants in Mississippi and Alabama. In the course of doing his work, he continued to garner the expertise he would need to build a winning team of his own.

"I was moved into plants and facilities that weren't doing well," he remembered. "They were inefficient or the quality was poor, and I was sent in to straighten them out. I learned pretty quickly that the important thing was trying to work with people and develop a team that could work together. I learned the importance of hiring and developing those folks."

But in 1979 Randy was faced with having to move to another city, which would have been the eighth move in only 13 years. As he considered his options, he knew that he had reached the end of his tolerance. Along with that, Randy could foresee that there wasn't going to be much of a future in the domestic clothing business.

THE GAME BEGINS

Randy and his wife, Charlene, heard about Service-Master through listening to Paul Harvey. Soon they obtained information about the possibility of buying a franchise and actually made two or three trips around the South just visiting ServiceMaster franchisees.

"We were really impressed with the 'family nature' of the businesses we saw," Randy recalled. "I was 39 years old, and I had always had a desire to be in business for myself. If I was going to have to make a career change, and if I was going to do something on my own, I knew I needed to do it then. I liked the training program and the track record of ServiceMaster. It looked like a good, sound company."

As he envisioned the business, he also realized that it would present a great opportunity for his whole family. "My son Chris, who was a sophomore in high school, and I cleaned my pastor's carpet here in town. It was the first job we ever had, and we did it together. I can see that I always had it in the back of my mind to build a family business—a business my sons could be involved in," Randy said.

Randy's first franchise, an on-location business in Columbus, Mississippi, began in May of 1979. Two years later he and Charlene added a Commercial Services business and then started another franchise operation, taking on Jim Black as a partner.

Today ServiceMaster Building Maintenance owns Commercial Service franchises in Memphis, Tennessee; Tupelo and Columbus, Mississippi; and in Tuscaloosa, Montgomery, and Birmingham, Alabama. They employ around 400 team members and have annual revenues that have placed them at the top.

"We recognized that we could achieve only so much market penetration within an area, so we didn't waste time by staying only in Columbus. We are in a rural area and most of our franchises are too," Randy said, "with the exception of Memphis and the one we just bought in Birmingham. We needed to continue to penetrate our market more and more, and also look in other market areas too while we grew our franchises."

Building a Team of Trained Technicians

When Randy first began his ServiceMaster career, he knew nothing about cleaning carpets. "I'll admit that I was intimidated by the technical aspect. I really studied and took the Academy of Service and training seriously. I studied my filmstrips and manuals. I wanted to be very strong technically and know as much as I could. You need to know what you're doing when you start cleaning furniture…or you are going to buy yourself a sofa, which I did," Randy said with a chuckle. "Although the technical aspect was intimidating, we knew we weren't building rockets; we just wanted to be comfortable doing the work."

Even though the beginning of the business represented the fulfillment of a desire he'd had since his youth, he had to fight against becoming discouraged. "I lost 30 pounds in the first six months of the business," Randy remembered, "just because of apprehension and worry. I used to lay in bed at night and pray. I didn't know anything about sales. 'Lord,' I would pray, 'if You sell it, I promise that I'll do my best to produce it better than anybody else.' That is why I've always been such a stickler for the technical aspect of it," Randy admitted. "I wanted to make sure I could clean better than anyone else."

AN EMPTY HAIRCUT ENVELOPE

When the business first started out, Randy's goal was merely to care for his family. Although his wife, Charlene, was teaching school, he can testify that Mississippi school-teachers aren't "overly compensated." Randy already knew the importance of financial controls and planning, so every month he and Charlene made out their budget.

"We would get cash money out of the bank and put it in envelopes. We had an envelope for haircuts, for clothing, for food, for entertainment, and so on. We allocated 'x' amount of money to each envelope," Randy remembered, "and, by golly, if the envelope was empty, that was it. If daddy got ready to have a haircut and that envelope was empty, he didn't get a haircut. That gives an idea of how tight it was. We had very little working capital. We operated the business out of our home, and our monthly budget was about $800. You can go back in my files, and I can guarantee you that we have 22 years of budgets and monthly financial statements."

Randy continues to have very strong opinions about maintaining financial controls in a business. "If you're going to be successful, you've got to live within your means," he stated emphatically. "You've got to have a budget and live in it. You've got to invest back into your business. If you don't have the reserves, you can't take advantage of the opportunities." And it is obvious that Randy and his team know all about taking advantage of business opportunities.

PUTTING TOGETHER A WINNING ROSTER

When he first started, Randy cherished the hope that the business would afford him the opportunity to build a team.

He's worked conscientiously during the last two decades to grow his business for the express purpose of providing a place where he could help people develop.

"I enjoy teamwork," Randy stated. "I'll admit that's my only strong suit. I have a lot of weaknesses, but the one thing I do like is to have a team, an organization. I really like to help people develop."

As Randy reflected on ServiceMaster's four corporate objectives, he laid out his basic business philosophy: He sees the first two objectives, Honoring God and Helping People Develop, as the end game. The last two, Pursuing Excellence and Growing Profitably, he sees as the game plan to achieve that end.

For instance, Randy stresses excellence of service in his business. In order to see that the team achieves that goal, he's put what might be called "player bonuses" in place. "We have bonus and recognition programs for all our employees. We survey our customers every quarter, asking them to judge us on how well we are serving their facility and meeting their needs. If we are judged well, the employees of that facility get a bonus that quarter. Last year we paid out thousands of dollars in bonus money."

"We're really trying to develop our people, and in doing that we also try to stress training. We bring in all our managers and have quarterly training sessions. These sessions aren't just on how to do floors, but relate directly to business operations, such as how to read financial statements. We've also brought in outside people who've talked about safety hazards and even sexual harassment in the workplace."

Randy explained his compensation programs: "Every division has a budget, and the division is accountable for that budget. There is also a performance-based compensation program. They can achieve substantial compensation for meeting or bettering their budget and helping the company to do the same. Last year we gave out thousands of dollars worth of management performance compensation bonuses.

In order to hold the managers accountable for their contribution to the company, we had to have an open-book policy with our managers. They have to see how their division contributes to and effects the company as a whole. At first we struggled with that, but if part of their compensation was to be based on how the company as a whole is doing, we had to do it. We had to educate them—it's just part of their growth and development. We try to encourage people who have the desire, ambition, and hunger to succeed."

In addition to their quality-recognition program, Randy and Charlene also recognize every manager who has achieved set budgetary goals, kept labor turnover low, retained current business, contributed to the overheads, and had no time lost due to injuries. Any manager who reaches any of these goals is recognized at their annual Christmas party.

THE PLAYER'S HALL OF FAME

McDonald Ezell joined the ServiceMaster Building Maintenance team in the early 1990s. First hired as a part-time supervisor, his leadership and conscientiousness soon opened the way for him to become the supervisor at a very large facility. "Mac" had a reputation for sincerely caring about both his clients and his employees. "He was just one of those guys that everyone liked very much; a real all-star. He treated people fairly, honestly, and openly; he was a fantastic guy. He wanted to try to live out the corporate objectives. He was a Christian man, a wonderful guy. He really cared about his clients and his employees," Randy remembered. "He was really loved."

Unfortunately, after only five years on the team, Mac had a untimely heart attack and passed away. "All of his employees and clients were at his funeral. I don't think that I have ever known of a manager who was loved like he was."

To honor the memory of this unique man, Service-Master Building Maintenance has set up the McDonald Ezell

Leadership Award. Every year one manager or supervisor is chosen who best exemplifies the qualities and character of this beloved team leader. "We don't want that name or what he stood for to be forgotten. He set the bar really high for managers, so this award is the top one that we give."

SPRING TRAINING

Once a year the company has a family retreat for every manager and his or her family. "We spend the weekend together at a state park. We have someone come in from the ServiceMaster Clean corporate offices in Memphis to conduct a session or two. But it is mostly just an opportunity for all of our managers and their families to interact and feel like they are a part of the whole team. I really find that very beneficial and enjoyable."

"I probably come across like a blubbering idiot when I start talking about the folks in my company," Randy confessed. "Maybe I am a little too proud of the family and the folks that are here. As the company has grown, with over 400 employees spread out over 50,000 square miles, the greatest sacrifice has been that I can't get to know each one of them personally."

POISED FOR THE PENNANT

In their conference room in Columbus, Mississippi, is a banner emblazoned with two words: *Integrity* and *Credibility*.

"I chose those words several years ago," Randy stated, "and they guide all our actions in our relationships with our employees and our clients. It is extremely important that as managers we have the trust of our employees, that they can believe what we tell them, and that we follow through. If we don't have the trust of our employees, we are going to be dead in the water. I tell folks that I don't believe that credibility and integrity will guarantee success, but I am sure that if we don't have them it will guarantee failure."

A DREAM COME TRUE

Randy's dream to field a team on which his sons could star has been fully realized. Both of his sons, Chris and John, are actively involved in ServiceMaster Building Maintenance. Chris is president and chief operating officer, and John is vice president for the state of Mississippi. Chris' wife, Stacy, is vice president of administration. Jim Black, Randy's partner from Tupelo, is now vice president of sales. When Chris asked his dad, Randy, if there were any opportunities in the business for he and his wife, Randy was overjoyed. "Boy," I said, "that is a dream come true."

Randy's career as a team manager will soon be drawing to a close. He knows that the crew that he's fielded will keep the business growing and prospering. Most of all, he knows that the business is in a great position to continue to offer opportunities for other people to grow. "With the synergism amongst the team members, I think that the business is in a good position. Owning your own business shouldn't be looked at as a get-rich-quick scheme," he said. "But, ServiceMaster offers a great opportunity for people who are willing to tighten up their belt and work hard. If you do, you'll be able to provide opportunities for other folks to grow and realize their dreams, too."

In 1989 Randy's business won the Marion E. Wade Master Award, which is ServiceMaster's way of saying that Randy McCall is a Most Valuable Player...and like all good managers, Randy would smile at that phrase and say, "It was really just a team effort."

PLOTTING OUT A WINNING STRATEGY

The Story of Charles A. and Alyce Horton

"We played to win, and as long as we continued to feel this way we were unbeatable..."
Marion E. Wade[1]

Although Charles Horton's introduction to ServiceMaster was through the company's hospital division in the early 1980s, he never really envisioned himself in the cleaning business. "I had no desire to ever be a part of a company that did cleaning, but I saw this opportunity to work for ServiceMaster as a chance to gain some managerial experience. Surprisingly, this was the very opportunity that permitted me to have my own business. So when I went to work for corporate, I went with the mindset of eventually starting a franchise and buying my own business, although I didn't know at the time how that dream would be fulfilled.

As a kid growing up, I had always talked about wanting to be self-employed…that had always been my focus."

Charles Horton's history begins in a small town north of Memphis, Tennessee. Ripley was home to Charles, his father A. D., his mother Ethel, and his nine older siblings. Although the family was not wealthy, Charles knows that these early years were important in the shaping of his future success.

"My father was a hard-working man," Charles recalls. "He was out and gone by 5:00 a.m. and never came home before 7:00 p.m. at night. He worked from sunup to sundown. That is all we ever knew."

Charles believes that his father was a success because he provided for everything the family needed, including all the food. "He raised all the meat. He had pigs, cows, horses, a garden, and an apple and peach tree. We had pecans, walnuts, and raspberries. He fed his family from his own farm. There was no reason to go to the grocery store and buy meat or vegetables because he raised it all for us. You know, he was truly an entrepreneur before his time. He was self-sufficient. He also helped other farmers find workers, and he was a handyman." It was during these early years, as Charles observed his father's independence and work habits, that his own desire to be an entrepreneur blossomed into a fully developed passion. "I had the desire as a kid to be self-employed…I just wasn't sure how."

LEAVING THE COUNTRY FOR THE CITY

But Charles' serene rural life changed radically when he was 10. His father, who was in his early seventies by that time, died of cancer. Upon his death, Charles' mother and sister decided to move north to Detroit and join the rest of the children, who were working in the automotive industry.

Charles remembers this move as a difficult time. Although the thought of moving to a big city was exciting, there were great obstacles to overcome. "There was a lot of stress on the family. It was difficult trying to make it on our own financially. My mom had never worked outside the home before because dad had always taken care of the household. But when he died, my mom had to go to work." Even at his young age, Charles knew that the three of them would have to be self-sufficient.

"At the age of 10 I felt I should get a job to take care of myself. If my mother was able to take care of herself, with my working, we would make it. So I got a job at a food market. After school, I would wipe off the tomatoes and apples and then package the fruit into a nice basket." Although Charles worked only two or three hours a day, it was a way for him to take care of himself. Charles used the money from his job to pay for his own expenses. "If I wanted special clothes or if there was a special activity at school, I paid the cost myself. It was just a way to keep my mother from having to care for me as a kid growing up." His mother did eventually find a job as a cook in a local school and was very active in a nearby church, attending several times a week. Charles' world was settling down.

One of Charles' older brothers was in real estate and gave him his first opportunity to explore what it was like being an entrepreneur. "At my brother's invitation, I invested in my first piece of real estate when I was 16. I had saved my money to buy a car, but instead I put the $1,000 into real estate. In one year's time I had a return of $2,800! That transaction afforded me the opportunity to see that I could make money. It pushed me to work more. I continued to buy property so that when the time came for me to go into business, I would be ready. That experience really excited me and reinforced my desire to be self-employed."

After graduating from high school, Charles attended Wayne State University, but decided in his third year that the path to his dreams laid elsewhere. He was driven by the desire to work and prepare for his future as a business owner, so he went out into the business world. Because his entire life was focused on this goal, he worked for seven years for the

Ford Motor Company, scrimping and investing every extra penny. The hours that he worked were long and hard, but from 1973 to 1977 he bought 20 houses, always planning and plotting for the time when he would leave Ford and go out on his own. He knew that the property he owned could be parlayed into self-sufficiency and independence. It was during these seven long years that he recalls telling his sister, "I am not going to work for a company all my life. One of these days I will work for myself." By this time, Charles' mantra was old hat to his family; after all, he had started saying things like that when he was only nine years old.

After leaving Ford, Charles worked for ServiceMaster until 1984 when he decided he was ready to go into business for himself. He resigned from ServiceMaster to start his business, but an incredible opportunity was presented to him at General Motors, so he put aside his dream and worked in management for GM for nine months. During that time he saved an extra $30,000 to invest in his business. "On September 13, I resigned from GM and started my business full time. From that day I have never looked back. It has been growth from one day to the next."

BACK TO THE COUNTRY

Although all his life Charles had planned to be a business owner, he didn't know exactly where that would take him. On one business trip, however, he had discovered the little town of Oberlin, Ohio. He admits that the reason he found it was because he was lost. He was just driving down a street, spotted a house, and parked in front of it, and thought about how he would like to live there. Later he came back and bought the house and moved to Oberlin in 1977.

Charles purposely selected Oberlin as his home because it was a small, rural town, similar to the one in which he had spent his early years in Tennessee. It had a population of only 5,600 and was primarily known for Oberlin College, a liberal arts school that specializes in music and art. As Charles stood on the threshold of his dream, he felt intimidated because he didn't know how the business world functioned in a small town. "I was brand new to the town and brand new as a minority trying to start a business. But I bought a franchise and was determined that the business was going to be successful." His wife, Alyce, was his first employee. In addition to her job with the Social Security Administration, she helped him manage the financial side of the business, and on some occasions, if Charles needed help, she would even go out on a job with him.

Charles remembers the first few years as demanding and yet rewarding. "I went downtown, parked my car, and did cold calls. I knocked on every door in the city of Oberlin. I introduced myself just to let folks know that I was starting a carpet, upholstery, and office-cleaning business. I told them to give me a call if I could help them sometime in the future. Within six months, I had worked for just about every customer I had called on. In fact, I still work for many of those same customers today. I have built a business from inside out. Most people buy a franchise in a large city where there are a lot of folks, but if you are in a small city, you don't really have a choice—you have to contact everyone."

"If you build a business from the inside out, you can dominate your market." That's just what Charles has done over the last 18 years. "We dominate the cleaning market in Oberlin and also in Elyria, which is 14 miles away. I spent the first five years working exclusively in Oberlin. I worked until I knew that anybody who wanted something done in Oberlin would call ServiceMaster. Then I started to take on jobs out of my area."

The Opportunity to Explore Your Own Limits

Charles brought an extraordinary work ethic with him into his franchise. Although he had worked hard for Ford, he knew that he didn't want to be confined to a factory five days

177

a week. As he reflected on his time there, he said, "You really have no opportunity to think for yourself. You have no opportunity to explore or grow." But working at Ford helped prepare him to face the challenges of business ownership. For one thing, the long hours that he had to work when he started his own business weren't a shock to him. "I have worked long hours my whole life. I've worked seven days a week, 10-12 hours a day. That training actually prepared me to be self-employed. Once I started my business it was seven days a week, 18 hours a day. I'm up at 3:00 a.m. plotting my strategy for the coming day. When a person wants to be self-employed and they have no idea of the amount of time involved, it can be frightening. Owning your own business sounds good, but it is a lot of work to make it successful."

OVERCOMING OBSTACLES BY
GIVING BACK TO HIS COMMUNITY

"When the average person starts a business he already has one major obstacle to overcome, and my being a minority doesn't help," Charles conceded. "When a minority starts a business, he has two built-in hurdles to go over."

In a small town like Oberlin, the "good ol' boy" network still exists. Charles knew that in order to be successful, he had to break into that network and even become part of it. "I found that being involved in many of the civic activities gave me an opportunity to be a part of the business world in Oberlin. I joined the local Exchange Club and the Rotary. Now I sit on the boards of the Oberlin Chamber of Commerce, the local hospital, the Community Foundation, and the Salvation Army. I am the chairman of the trustees of my church. I've purposely set out to make myself very visible in the community. My involvement in the community has helped my business grow because the folks that I meet with each month have asked me to do cleaning jobs for them. Many of the presidents of the local businesses were members of the Rotary or Exchange Club, and that's how I became acquainted with them. I appreciate living in a small town because it's given me the opportunity to establish good relationships with people. I'm really a small-town country boy."

Charles believes that success is also defined by how much one gives back to the community. He sees that building a business and giving of your time to the community works hand in hand with each other. "There will always be obstacles, but you cannot let that stop you from growing your business," Charles stated emphatically. "I have always found a way to go over or under any obstacle. For instance, when I first started my business I found that there was another company pursuing the same customers. I wasn't getting the business. Our prices were the same, but I discovered that because I was a minority in the house-cleaning business, I wasn't getting the calls. For me, that was just one more obstacle to overcome. So, I bought out the other company. I bought the owner out, and she came to work for me. We continued to pursue the same customers under their name, only the customers didn't know that I owned the business. You see," Charles said reflectively, "you have to constantly challenge yourself if you're going to make your business a success. You have to be determined. My goal has always been to be number one, and I've had to think of unique ways to accomplish that."

SUCCESS THROUGH EXCELLENCE

Charles recognizes that the only way to pursue the number-one position in his market is by teaching his staff to consistently do the very best they can. It has always been his goal to have a company that is the best at what it does. In order to accomplish this end, he diligently teaches his people what his operation is about and how it has arrived in its present position. He recognizes that he can't be on every job every day, so he inculcates into his managers and crew chiefs the responsibility to stress quality and pursue excellence. "To be number one you've got to do a quality job, and you've got to do it in a timely manner," Charles stated definitively. "For me, that's what it means to honor God in our work."

For Charles, the secret of success is in wanting to be successful and then striving with all one's heart to make it happen. Charles believes that there are opportunities out there for everyone who wants to be successful, "but you have to dedicate the time and the effort to make it happen. It doesn't come and knock on your door. You have to go and get it. You have to make yourself successful. You have to work at it, learn the system, and make it work for you."

Another obstacle that Charles had to overcome has been that of finding good employees. So Charles searched out young men who shared his work ethic. He eventually found Stuart and David, young men who had spent years in other companies, and recruited them as managers. He hired them with the prospect that they would eventually own their own franchises. "I told them that I would teach them how to run a business and then help them buy their own. We eventually purchased another franchise about 25 miles from Oberlin that the three of us own. Stuart is the operations manager of that business, and David is part owner. David has decided to stay in my business, and when I retire, David will take it over."

Passing On the Vision to Others

Charles has a vision to encourage and pursue minorities with the goal of convincing them to become franchise owners. He wants to reach out and spread the message of opportunity to them. "I want to let people who are in communities like the one I grew up in on the east side of Detroit to know that they can grow a business. I know that they think that people who are successful in business have a lot of money from the start, but I know that's not the truth. All you need is the desire to be successful, and you can make it happen. My father, A. D. Horton, was a farmer, but in my book, he was a success."

Has Charles followed in his father's footsteps and become a success? Of course. In 1999, he was voted Businessman of the Year in all of Loraine County, Ohio. He was also named one of the top 30 businesses (out of 1500) by the Chamber of Commerce. His business ranked third in 1999 and sixth in 2000. From childhood, Charles has pursued his dream to be self-sufficient, self-employed, and self-reliant. Charles' employs over 200 people and is one of the top businesses in the ServiceMaster Clean family. Like his father before him, Charles Horton has achieved his goal of self-sufficiency, community involvement, and success. He believes that's a goal that is attainable for anyone who really wants to pursue it—no matter what their background.

"WHY DO YOU DO THIS?"

The Story of Evelyn Brown

"I found myself wondering what the Lord would do with a company that was entirely His...in which every employee did his job for the glory of God."

Marion E. Wade[1]

The concrete floor was cold beneath Evelyn Brown as she sat Indian-style, polishing the chrome at the base of the door before her. Her legs ached below her. Her arms and shoulders felt as though she were holding an anvil, rather than a weightless cleaning cloth. All her attention was focused on the task before her.

This chore was just one in what seemed like endless days filled with chores. Evelyn's days were long—16-20 hours long. She labored hour after hour cleaning and instructing other employees. She was alone and bone-tired. She was so intent on the task before her that she didn't notice Louis, a new employee, watching her. Finally he couldn't contain his curiosity any longer. "Evelyn, why do you do this?," he asked. Exhausted and weary, Evelyn's determination dissolved into tears.

When a business is in its beginning stages, owners usually bear the brunt of the manual labor. So, perhaps the little vignette above doesn't seem too impressive to you. It should. Evelyn Brown, the cleaning woman on the floor on this particular Sunday night, isn't a new business owner or even a manager. Evelyn Brown is the owner of ServiceMaster by Brown, a janitorial business that is among the top ten in the ServiceMaster family and employs 240. This isn't a story from the beginning of their business in 1980; no, it's a story from the summer of 2000.

What motivates Evelyn? Is it simply the desire to build a profitable business? Or is it something deeper? Is her primary concern the bottom line, or is there within her heart an inspiration to do something more? To understand Evelyn's motives, you have to look into her background, into her fundamental core beliefs. Evelyn isn't the graduate of a renowned business school nor the heir of a fortune from her family. No, the education and inheritance that she brought into her business had its genesis in her childhood training—training that she received in her home and her church.

Raised in a Plymouth Brethren congregation, Evelyn and her husband, David, have been sweethearts all their lives. They were raised together in the same little church, and when she was a child he used to carry her around the church on his back. So, it seemed natural that they would marry, and when she was 17, they tied the knot. Evelyn loves the fact that David's been "sweet on her all her life."

As a young woman, she looked ahead to a life with David no different than her mother's: taking in ironing to make ends meet, watching her family grow. Evelyn recalls her mother's labors: "I remember sitting on the bed talking to her and learning my life values while I watched her iron for people." Any questions that Evelyn had about why her mother did what she did were answered in those early years, watching her serve and work diligently for others.

Among the members of the Plymouth Brethren congregation, it was unheard of for a woman to work outside the home, and Evelyn envisioned a distinct path marked out for her, as a Christian, as a woman. She would raise her children, work in the church, and serve her family. Both David and Evelyn had been taught to do one thing in life: serve. They believed in a service ethic, but had no notion of how that ideal would be the Polar Star of an existence very different from their parents'. They would become *masters of service,* and their new business would offer them more opportunities to serve than they could have ever imagined.

"We believed that serving and accommodating others was the only way to find happiness. We both believed that we couldn't be happy and fulfilled unless we were serving. For us, service is a family way of life. As I've gotten older I've learned that the business is a way to serve. Our belief and our foundation in serving the Lord and other people was a part of who we were. When we discovered that ServiceMaster had the same values and character beliefs that we had, we knew it would be the right fit for us."

Evelyn and David first considered purchasing a ServiceMaster franchise in the early 1980s after listening to Paul Harvey on the radio. She was a housewife with three children in the home, and he worked for the local power company. There was a franchise license for sale in the Albuquerque area, and since that locale was one that had always interested them, they decided through prayer and Bible study to take the leap. But starting a service business wasn't really that much of a leap for Evelyn because she had been taught to serve others her whole life.

In 1980 they moved to Albuquerque with less than $6,000 in the bank. This money had to stretch to feed five mouths and operate the business until a cash flow could be generated. Evelyn reminisced about those early days: "Both of us were working day and night. It was good that we were both raised with a very strong work ethic. We both did proposals, and I did the accounting and ran the business and clerical side. Dave helped with the mops and towels and all the production. He trained the floor men, and I trained the housekeeping staff."

At first, Evelyn handled the business from home, and Dave oversaw the production. But, as the production side became more demanding, Evelyn began to sell jobs while continuing to run the office. It was here that Evelyn found her niche. She found that she loved to sell. She loved having the opportunity to convince people that she represented a company that offered a service they really needed. She enjoyed seeing them change their mind from being very set on what they thought they wanted to seeing it her way.

"How Do You Spell Success?"

Like all young business owners, Dave and Evelyn first equated success with building a "big business." But as the years have passed they have discovered that the relationships that they have built through the business have been the true measure of their accomplishments.

"There is no substitute for building the proper kinds of relationships" Evelyn declared. "I think a lot of people go into business thinking that dollars and acclaim and recognition are going to make them happy. But, after being in business for 20 years, I can say what is really meaningful are the relationships we have built."

For Evelyn, relationships flow out of the foundational ethics that inform her every decision. "I want to be able to look back over my relationships with my employees and my customers and be able to say, 'I made a difference in that person's life.' It's so tempting to just look at the monetary side of what this business can do for us. There is no substitute for the development of people and the relationships we can build with them. If we accomplish that, the building of strong ethical relationships, everything else will fall into place: the profitability, and the excellence."

Conversely, the Browns recognize there is a continuous tension between the financial and the personal in business. Because their profit margins in commercial cleaning are so narrow, deciding between fiscal prudence and the subjective needs of individuals is often difficult. "This business has not always been as profitable as I would have liked it to be, but I can say that the relationships have been solid and strong. There are a lot of years of history in my business with my employees and to me *that is success.*"

The belief that the individual's needs are as important as the corporation's has been Evelyn's conviction. Because of this she has had the joy of watching the impact that her brand of ethical relationships with employees can have. She's literally watched workers begin as bathroom cleaners and move up into management positions. She's celebrated the changes in their lifestyles because of the opportunities their business relationship afforded them.

"How Am I Ever Going to Buy a Home?"

In the late 1980s Susan came to work for ServiceMaster by Brown. Susan started out as a part-time housekeeper, working in the evening. Although she was in her forties, she had never owned a home of her own. On one occasion, she came to Evelyn and asked, "How am I ever going to be able to buy my own home? I have my job with you, but I need to live on the wages that I bring home." As Evelyn evaluated her home-buying prospects, she saw that she was right in her assessment.

"We wanted to help her find a way to buy a home," Evelyn remembers. "So we set up a stock purchase program for her and promised that after she committed a certain amount of money to purchase stock, the business would respond by committing so much. After four years, she sold her stock and had enough money to put a down payment on a home."

Susan has worked for Evelyn for more than 12 years, although she's no longer a part-time housekeeper. She's now an operations manager and has five other managers working under her supervision. She oversees the entire nighttime operation and makes sure that each customer is served. Her relationship with Evelyn and ServiceMaster by Brown has changed her life forever.

"CAN YOU SERVICE OUR NEW BUSINESS...IN CALIFORNIA?"

ServiceMaster by Brown has this level of relationship with their customers as well. One business has used their cleaning services for over 20 years. During this time, it has won award after award for excellence in quality. So it was no surprise that when they decided to open a division in California, they knew who to hire for their cleaning services. In response to their request, Evelyn's service ethic even prompted her to leave her comfortable home in New Mexico for nine weeks so that she could set up crews at the 19-acre facility in Los Angeles.

"WHO IS GOING TO KNOW?"

Through the years, ServiceMaster's four corporate objectives have kept Evelyn focused when she might have become discouraged or been tempted to let her values slip. Recently after negotiating with a customer on a contract, the customer sent the contract back to her for signature. When she read it she found a very profound error in her favor had been made.

"I would have gained about $2500 a month because of the way they wrote the contract," she said. "It was clearly not what we had talked about." So she informed her contact at the company, "I don't want to sign this. This isn't right."

Stunned, but intrigued by her principled stance, he asked, "Why don't you just go ahead and sign it? Who is going to know?"

For Evelyn, the question wasn't one of expediency or even who might catch her. It was a test of the ethics and foundational character that informs all her decisions. "I'm going to know," she told him. "It isn't right. This isn't right, and I will know."

In the cutthroat world of commercial cleaning, unscrupulous dealings are commonplace and expected. But for Evelyn, there is a higher watermark than popular morals. "It is hard to claim that you follow the corporate objectives if you have done something unethical." Even so Evelyn admits that "the tough part is that our competitors do play these kinds of games and so, to some degree, that is the expectation of our clients. To retain integrity and ethics is sometimes difficult with the temptations that we are faced with. But the objectives help keep me focused."

"WHERE'S OUR REFRIGERATOR?"

Through the years, the clients of ServiceMaster by Brown have repeatedly defined their business using the word, *integrity*. When her customers use that word, they mean something more than fulfilling responsibilities or even refusing to sign incorrect contracts. Honesty and honor pervade every aspect of the operation. "When my employees ram vacuum cleaners into walls or break pictures or shatter expensive vases, I don't make any bones about our responsibility," Evelyn says. Rather than quibble with her clients about responsibility, she unhesitatingly admits that she is certain her employees are culpable and sets about replacing or repairing the item. ServiceMaster by Brown is set apart from their competition because they never hide their mistakes. "If I know that an employee damaged or broke something in a building, then I call the client and tell them about it. I don't wait for them to call me or try to deny it."

Recently, Evelyn received a report that a small refrigerator had turned up missing from one of her job sites. After speaking with the nighttime manager, who then spoke to the employee on the job, they determined that the employee had, indeed, taken it. In fact, it was still in the employee's car. They told the employee to get it and bring it back to the building. Evelyn realized how it must have looked to have her employee walk through the building with the stolen merchandise. But she and her management team knew that something more than momentary embarrassment was at stake. Her company's reputation, and her personal integrity were in jeopardy. "Other businesses would probably have denied responsibility or tried to sweep the problem under the rug. It certainly would have looked better for us if we had. I don't do business that way."

How Will Future Service Look?

In 1989 Dave purchased a ServiceMaster distributorship that he sold back to ServiceMaster Clean in 1997. Since then he's worked for the home office as a market manager. The Browns' daughter has worked in management in the business and is now raising a family of her own, inculcating the service ethic into her children.

The Browns' heart to serve hasn't been fully tapped out yet, though. Once they retire, they plan to open a bed-and-breakfast in Washington state, where they've already purchased 12 acres.

As Evelyn reminisced about the early days in the business, she recognized that those closest to her and Dave frequently doubted their chances for success. They were told that they were too young to start a business. They were reminded that they didn't know anything about running a business and had no connections. In addition, Evelyn had to break through gender-based barriers; she ran the business, she sold service contracts. And as Dave became more and more involved in his distributorship, the business became, for all intents and purposes, Evelyn's.

Although it might have seemed to some that the Browns had moved away from their Christian moorings, the truths that they were taught as children continue to inform and enlighten everything they do today. "I think it is a testament for when God is in something," Evelyn stated emphatically. "He can make you a success, even when it seems impossible."

"EVELYN, WHY DO YOU DO THIS?"

When Louis inquired into Evelyn's motivation on that Sunday night, Evelyn spoke from her heart. "Just give me a few minutes to pull myself together, and I'll answer you," she said. "But first, I want you to tell me what you mean by that question."

"You have a business back home, and you have employees," Louis stated. "Why did you move out here? Why are you sitting on the floor cleaning that door?"

"Well, Louis, all I can say is when I leave here there will not be one thing that I will expect you to do that I haven't done myself," Evelyn answered. "So if I call and need you to do something for this customer, it is something I would do myself. I would never ask you to do anything that I wouldn't do myself."

Louis' reaction to Evelyn's answer was a quiet "Wow." It should be obvious that Louis' amazement isn't the first time that employees, clients, or peers have discovered Evelyn's nature and had that response. ServiceMaster by Brown is a reflection of the ethics and dedication to others that pervades every aspect of Evelyn Brown's character. "Wow" does seem like the best way to respond, doesn't it?

STEWARDSHIP: ONE TRADITION, FOUR GENERATIONS

The Clark Family Story

"A man is as accountable to God for his steward-ship in the ministry of business as much as in the ministry of being a husband or father."
Marion E. Wade[1]

When Myron Clark came into the ServiceMaster Clean family, he had already completed several successful careers and was nearing what for most people would have been the time to consider retirement.

FROM DAIRY COWS TO PERRY COMO

As a young man growing up on a 70-acre farm in Minnesota, Myron was given a young purebred calf by his father. His father told him that if he would raise the calf, all her female offspring would be his. He could then use that stock to build a herd of his own. After graduating from college, he started farming and thought that he "had the world by the tail." But within a short time the entire herd of 40 Holstein cows had contracted an infectious disease and had to be sold for dog food. He had earned barely enough money to fund their transport to market. "Sounds like time for a prayer meeting, don't you think?" Myron quipped as he remembered his predicament.

Soon a friend approached Myron about raising cattle for him and made a deal with him. In exchange for Myron caring for the cows, they would split the proceeds from the milk. Over the course of the next 18 years, Myron built an award-winning herd of purebred cattle that he sold across the nation and in three foreign countries. Myron had made a reputation for himself in the dairy industry.

In 1950 Myron was enlisted by then-Minnesota governor Luther W. Youngdahl and appointed to be the commissioner of the Department of Agriculture. As commissioner, Myron administered the programs of the Department of Agriculture, set policy directions for the agency and served as a spokesman for Minnesota agriculture throughout the state and nation.

GOT MILK?

Myron accepted a position in 1956 as the membership director for the National Dairy Farmer's Association, a new entity that sought to pool the resources of dairy farmers for concerted advertising efforts. He helped develop the first national advertising campaigns for dairy products and hired Perry Como to be the Association's representative.

By the mid-1960s, Myron had quite an accomplished career in dairy farming and related fields. It was then that Ken Hansen, a friend Myron knew from his Sunday school class, and Ed Morgan, a neighbor and friend, introduced Myron to the young business then known as Wade, Wenger and Associates. After a conference with Marion Wade, Myron was hired by the company to work in market expansion and to assist in forging relationships within the insurance industry. A family lifestyle that would impact four generations was begun.

DOORS OPEN ON A SUNDAY

Part of Myron's job was to try to build connections with adjusters in the insurance industry, but initially he wasn't very successful at it. "I just couldn't get in the front door," Myron remembers. In 1965, while visiting the New York's World's Fair, he found himself in front of an edifice entitled "Insurance Adjusters Building." Although it was Sunday, and he didn't really expect anyone to be at work, he knocked on the door. Surprisingly, a fellow answered who turned out to be one of the leaders of the organization. Myron introduced himself and told him about ServiceMaster and the company's desire to do disaster restoration work for insurance adjusters. The gentleman kindly gave Myron the names and telephone numbers of insurance contacts across the nation. More importantly, he also gave him permission to use his name as an entree into the industry, and doors began to open for ServiceMaster's disaster restoration business.

REACHING ACROSS THE PACIFIC

After an all-night flight to vacation at the World's Fair in Japan in 1970, Myron was approached at his hotel by representatives of the Duskin Company, a Japanese franchising firm that had been investigating in the possibility of joining forces with ServiceMaster. After having dinner, a short time of discussion and some socializing, Myron left the group and retired to his room. The next day they held more discussions, as well as a time of prayer and more socializing. Finally, in frustration because he was supposed to be in Japan on vacation with his wife, he decided that he'd better push his hosts for a decision. Although they seemed to be offended by this brash demand, after two hours they returned to the room with signed contracts.

When Myron returned home to Chicago and the home offices of ServiceMaster, one of the office workers said that they were sorry that he had wasted his vacation time in Japan, since the Japanese had informed the corporate officers that they weren't interested in doing business. "But," Myron countered, "I have signed contracts." Needless to say, Ken Hansen and the other top executives were pleasantly astounded. And so, Duskin and ServiceMaster formed an alliance that has lasted over 30 years and resulted in over 800 franchise owners.

THE SECOND-GENERATION CHARADE

Myron continued working for the corporation and also became partners with Lloyd Lenn in a distributorship in the Rochester, Minnesota area. Myron's son, Don, was working for Univac (later to become Unisys) in various management positions. In 1974 Don decided that it might be time to take a look around at other opportunities. Although he was interested in the opportunities available in ServiceMaster, he knew that his father wore "rose-colored glasses" when it came to the business. Don wanted to get the real scoop.

"I had reached a point in Univac where I didn't want my boss's job, and the politics were getting difficult. I wanted to be in charge of my own destiny, and ServiceMaster was pretty attractive," Don recalled. So he and a friend contacted ServiceMaster and asked for a meeting to discuss the possibility of purchasing a franchise. Because Don didn't want his father to try to influence his decision, he made the appointment using an alias: Tom Foster.

"Tom" and his friend met for lunch with a representative from ServiceMaster and, after the interview, he had made two decisions. First, he decided that he didn't want to go into business with his friend, and secondly, he decided that he wanted to pursue his future with ServiceMaster. Soon, "Tom" was contacted by his father, and he knew his charade had been discovered. "I don't know how my father found out about it, but he contacted me and said that if I was truly interested I should look at an opportunity in Rochester, Minnesota."

The decisions were made, and in August of 1974 Don purchased a cleaning business in Rochester. He began by building the on-location business and then tried to build the commercial services and distributorship side as well. During this difficult time he suffered some personal difficulties and ended up facing single parenthood, trying to raise four children, ranging in age from 5-15 years old.

Don remembers those early days as being very taxing. "I was trying to build three businesses and raise the children. I had to do all of those things at the same time. I just had to," Don remembers. "What sustained me during this time was faith, prayer and belief in the Lord and in the ServiceMaster system. Sometimes suffering is introduced into our lives to bring us closer to God. It happened to me, my father, and now my son, too."

Don has amusing memories of the early days of the business and some of the founders' unusual conduct. For instance, in the mid-1980s Ken Hansen invited all the distributors and their wives into a room for a special meeting. There was only one problem: Ken had purposely not furnished them with any chairs.

"Ken proceeded to give us a lesson on finances, and we had to stand up the whole time," Don recalled with a smile. "The lesson lasted about one-and-a-half hours! It was a long time for people to stand, but I believe that Ken thought that we would pay attention better to a dull subject like that if we were standing."

Success Redefined

"When I first started out, I defined success as 'making enough money so that I could feed my family and survive,'" Don stated. "Then it was having enough money to send the kids to college. In 1976 I met a wonderful young lady, Dorrie, and we dated for a year. We were married in February of 1977. She already had a little boy, Jason, whom I adopted, and we merged the two families together. Now we had five children to care for. I can never say enough about how she held our family together through some pretty rough times," Don reminisced. "Now we are enjoying retirement together, and we have 11 grandchildren. The Lord has blessed us."

"As the years went on, my definition of success gradually changed. It started to change over to helping people develop and making a positive influence in other people's lives. I think I still feel that way. Success is the difference you make in people's lives, which is more significant than any financial gains you make."

In 1976, Don began purchasing distributorships in other areas. Beginning with Cedar Rapids, Iowa, he bought territories in Wisconsin, Illinois, Minnesota and South Dakota. In 1997, when Don retired, his distributor business had 172 franchises with remarkable annual revenues.

SERVICE MAY BE AN OVERUSED TERM

In 1979 Don sold his on-location business, and two years later he sold the commercial services business. This allowed him to concentrate fully on building the distributorship and on offering quality service to all his franchisees.

"*Service* may be an overused term," Don admitted, "but I think it is the word that best describes my role as a distributor. Service to the franchise owners is what makes the distributor's contribution valuable. This service can be on any level—financial counseling, sales training, and management training—all of the things that will give them the tools they need to help them grow their business. I realized that the people who were buying franchises had come from every kind of background, and most of them didn't have any idea of what it meant to be an entrepreneur. I see service as the mandate to work with them, help them through the bad times, and even to help them manage their wealth."

Don saw his obligation to provide service as a expanding mandate. In 1980 he was elected to the Idea Review Council, an association of ServiceMaster business owners and distributors. "We met in Chicago and were privy to some new programs. I felt like I was being exposed to the cutting edge of our business. Being involved like that gave me a good feeling."

So in 1985, Don instituted the same sort of program in his distributorship and called it the Advisory Council. "We invited franchise owners to come to our office in Rochester, where we spent time trying to find out what we could do to help and serve them better. I saw person after person take hold of this opportunity. Later on we decided to make the Advisory Council self-governing, and the franchisees elected their own chairperson. In the past the franchisees had indicated that they felt like they were isolated—like a little guy in a small town, that they didn't make much difference in the universe. Now they felt like they had a voice. The Advisory Council helped us establish many new programs. It also helped owners emerge who would then serve as leaders in other capacities. It was great to watch that grow, and the Advisory Council became a model for the way that we did business."

THE LEGACY IS PASSED ON

Don's son, Ed had his first introduction to ServiceMaster at a very early age. As his father's business grew, he was given the responsibility of washing the vans every weekend. He was also in charge of washing and folding the towels that were used in the business. The youngest child, with three older sisters, Ed frequently found himself working for his sisters. They contracted to pay him thirty cents an hour to clean their accounts. He remembers washing toilets at the local theater while his sisters chatted with their friends.

When Ed was seven, his grandfather struck a deal with him to encourage him in his stewardship. For every dollar that Ed saved to purchase ServiceMaster stock, his grandfather Myron would match it. By the time he was 10, he had saved $2000 by washing vans and working for his three older sisters. Even though the amount was a shock for his grandfather, Myron kept his word and matched it. Ed invested his money and then used the profits from the sale of the stock to pay for part of his tuition fees at college. At the age of ten, the handwriting was already on the wall: Ed was at home in the world of entrepreneurs.

DREAMS OF HIS OWN

As a young man, Ed didn't appreciate the opportunity within the family business. Let's face it, a cleaning business isn't very glamourous to a 17-year-old. Ed had firsthand experience with cleaning, and he was sure that it wasn't the life he wanted to pursue. So, he went to college and earned a degree majoring in Speech Communication and minoring in Business. He was ready to tackle the world and pursue his dreams.

Ed worked for a season in a marketing capacity for several companies in Minneapolis. He thought that the lifestyle found in a big city would be exciting and fulfilling. But he was soon bored and found that the desire to have in his own business was what really intrigued him. The entrepreneurial bug is hard to get out of your blood, especially when it is a couple of generations deep.

SHOW ME THE MONEY!

Ed admits that at first his motivation was purely financial. He saw money as the key to happiness and was driven by all the worldly desires and concerns that occupy young entrepreneurs. "I wanted to be successful and earn a lot of money," Ed concedes. Ed was busy building his own kingdom, but experience and time have changed his focus.

"I have come to see the light that the real reward for me in this business is the people I get to work with. I have had some unbelievable mentors from my organization and from the franchisees that I serve. These are people who embody the four corporate objectives. The way that they have mentored me has been the biggest benefit that I've been blessed with in this business."

"THE BOSS'S SON"

Although many might envy Ed's position, the truth is that as a 26-year-old it was tremendously difficult for him to walk into his father's highly successful business and assume management with no credibility of his own.

"You start out in the hole because you're the boss's kid," Ed acknowledges. "Right away everyone assumes that you have your job because it was a birthright. People don't like that. So I had to work very hard for several years to overcome that perception. I had to develop relationships with each of the people I worked alongside of in my dad's business, and with the franchisees I served. I worked hard to develop my skills and show people that even though I was given this opportunity because my dad was the boss, I wanted them to judge me on my own performance."

Ed spent the first few years just traveling to franchises and observing his father's interaction with the owners. He learned as he watched the questions he would ask and the direction he would take. "Over time, my position in the distributorship just naturally fell into place. I suppose that I gained credibility because of my desire to be honest. I don't have hidden agendas, and if I find myself in a situation that I don't have the answer for, I just admit it. That's something I learned from my father. He's an open book, a very transparent guy. Nobody ever wonders what he is thinking."

Although Ed still feels inadequate, especially in dealing with older franchisees, others have encouraged him to be confident in his level of skill. A few years ago one of his franchisees told him, "Ed, you greatly underestimate the influence you have with the franchisees." "I guess maybe I am not living up to my potential to develop other people because of my own insecurity. It's my goal to grow in this role, and I'm putting my whole passion into it."

NEW TREASURES: FAITH-BASED STEWARDSHIP

Life has not always been rosy for Ed. In fact, some days were a difficult exercise in putting one foot in front of another. During the past few years he's gone through some personal difficulties, but due to the character of his friends in ServiceMaster, his faith has been awakened, honed, and vitalized, and he's grown as a leader and a Christian. Ed's faith is now the defining focus of his life.

"The transformation within me has probably been the single biggest benefit that I have received from this business," Ed gratefully admits. "That's the number-one thing about this company: the character of the people in it. I know that's kind of a cliche, but in our company it's the truth. This is a unique organization of disciplined and moral people. For instance, people in other companies don't genuinely celebrate when their peers win an award or recognition. But in ServiceMaster they do because they really care about them. I just think that's so cool."

Ed's definition of success has changed over the years as well. "For me, success has become how well I lead the people that I serve. I am successful if the people that I lead feel that I am leading them well. I measure my success in their satisfaction and in the admiration and respect or fondness for me that they feel. I feel it in words that don't have to be spoken. It's evident whether they admire or respect me, or whether they think that I am a good steward of my position with them. I can see it in their eyes...and when I do, I know I'm being successful."

Ed sees stewardship as the foremost calling in his life. "Stewardship is basically acknowledging the responsibility that I have with the resources and leadership opportunities that I've been given. It involves helping others develop spiritually and cultivating the abilities that I've been given."

CHESS PIECES IN A PLAN

As Ed reflects on the course his life has taken, he admits that sometimes he is overwhelmed with awe. "I look at the way that I've been blessed and the things I've been given, and I wonder what the purpose of it is. It can't all be for me." He views every facet of his life as part of an overall plan with every piece fitting neatly into place on a great chessboard.

In recent years Ed has been involved with the people at Ironwood Springs Christian Ranch in Stewartville, Minnesota. Ironwood Springs is a nonprofit, nondenominational, year-round camp that serves over 20,000 people annually. Their mission is to provide an atmosphere and opportunity for adults and children "to get to know themselves, others and God better." Just last year the directors of Ironwood Springs asked Ed to serve on their advisory board, and he gladly accepted.

"I have always had this in my heart. The more material goods that I have been given, the more that I have realized that those things have nothing to do with happiness. They are just things, and they're just temporary. All the wealth in the world doesn't replace the friendships and the love and faith." Ed then reflected on the recent changes in his heart: "You know, it's funny when you realize that. I'm just thankful that I've realized it already." The measure of personal success is now a question of stewardship: "How can I use what I've been given for something other than my own selfish wants and desires?"

When Ed's son Lucas was born, some of his franchisees said to him, "Someday that boy is going to run your business." But Ed admits that when Lucas was first born he never saw that as a possibility. But now that he's five and starting school, Ed is seeing leadership qualities and ability. He's wondering if someday little Lucas will say to him, "Dad, do you have any room in that company for me?" We all know what the answer to that question will be!

ServiceMaster: A Way of Life

"ServiceMaster has become a way of life for our family," Don stated. "My father, Myron, is still a stockholder and vitally interested in what is going on. It is rewarding to see my son, Ed, with his son, Lucas working in the business. Lucas is washing trucks just like Ed did when he was that age. So now we have our fourth-generation entry-level employee. Our daughter Carolyn's husband is a part-owner of an on-location business in Minneapolis. Our family has lived and breathed ServiceMaster since my father started in the business in the 1960s. We developed our business to be the largest revenue-producing distributor in the system, with the most franchises."

From a small, but high-caliber, dairy farm in Minnesota to a government position, to a struggling franchise and now to an amazing success story, ServiceMaster has been the defining focus for all four generations. Myron, Don, Ed, and Lucas have found that faith in God and a high service ethic has enabled them to realize their dreams. These dreams didn't consist of mere financial independence, although they have certainly achieved that. Rather, they were visions of helping people develop and use their good fortune to be a blessing to their family and others.

An Abundance to Steward for the Advancement of Others

The spirit of ServiceMaster's founder, Marion Wade, lives in people like the Clarks. Although like Marion they've been greatly blessed materially, they've also correctly evaluated the purpose of their resources. "We have such great abundance," Ed admitted. "We have all been blessed so far beyond our needs and our wants. In some ways for me now it's a game. The game is, 'How can I help people and be a good steward of what I have been given?'"

THE PEOPLE
WE TOUCH

The Story of Mike and Jinny Isakson

*"No matter how big a company is, it is a single
unit and each employee has his own identity..."*
Marion E. Wade[1]

M ike Isakson is the president and chief operating
officer of the Franchise Services Group, which
includes Furniture Medic and ServiceMaster Clean, and he
oversees 5,000 franchises worldwide. But he didn't start out
in the corporate world. His leadership abilities have been
developed from childhood, a childhood that began unpre-
tentiously in Minnesota, as one of the five children of Ed and
Mary Louise Isakson, who were both schoolteachers.

Mike's first steps toward ServiceMaster began when
Dave Thiessen, Sr., started to lead the Boy's Christian Service
Brigade at Calvary Baptist Church in St. Cloud, Minnesota.

Dave might have noticed a little third grade boy in the group named Mike Isakson. Dave had just moved to St. Cloud from Duluth and was starting a ServiceMaster business. He owned a service business and was also the distributor for Central Minnesota and North Dakota.

Mike warmly remembers Dave's influence in his life. "Dave was the second Christian man to influence my life (after my father). All through junior and senior high, I was involved in his Brigade at church, and he was instrumental in helping me develop. Once in a while, he would ask me to help him at ServiceMaster on fire jobs or doing janitorial work. The first checks that I ever earned as a young person were from him."

Both of Mike's parents were teachers, and his wife Jinny's father was the principal of the high school. "I married the principal's daughter," Mike quipped. "My father was quiet but committed—a 'still waters run deep' kind of man. My mother was an organizer. They both had a strong faith and a potent desire to help young people develop."

Once Mike graduated from high school, he worked for a trucking company and earned a degree in Industrial Education and Special Ed. Mike spent a few more years with the trucking company, but soon learned that the opportunity to expand his position with the company was going to be stymied because he wasn't a member of the owner's family. "I just didn't have the right last name," he recalled.

"Why Don't You Go to Work for Yourself?"

So in 1977, Mike talked with his friend and mentor, Dave Theissen, about the possibility of working for him. Dave said, "Why don't you go to work for yourself?"

As Mike and Jinny mulled over the possibility of owning their own franchise, he recalled his family's experiences with in-home cleaning services. "I remembered what a big deal it was when we got the living room carpet cleaned. With five children in the home, you can imagine how it needed it. ServiceMaster was the company that had done the work. What an incredible experience it was to have someone come to our house and clean the carpet. And from my association with Dave, I knew that there were people who actually paid to have their homes and offices cleaned. So, Dave flew me out to Bismarck, North Dakota and talked me into buying a franchise."

Mike and Jinny decided to buy an on-location and contract services business, ServiceMaster of Central North Dakota. Then, in 1989, they purchased a Merry Maids franchise. When they eventually sold their businesses to join the Merry Maids staff, they employed 20 full time and 160 part-time people, and had superb market penetration.

Mike was drawn to ServiceMaster because he was well acquainted with Dave Theissen's character. "Dave defined his success in terms of who he was and how he lived. I also saw the merit of the franchisees, and that appealed to me. The quality of men like fellow franchise owner Bob Groff," (who has joined him in the home office staff,) "made me want to be part of ServiceMaster. The organization had such high standards. In addition, I recognized that the service industry was an industry that was going straight up."

As Mike and Jinny considered entrepreneurship, Mike recognized that without Jinny's involvement, the business wouldn't make it. "We both agreed that buying the business was the right thing to do, and that we were going to do it together. The business that we purchased in Bismarck was failing simply because the owner's spouse wasn't supportive. So we joined hands and Jinny took care of all the accounting and administrative work. There were times when she was just inundated with little kids and work, so her parents, Chuck and Cathy Sell, would come and help her out."

COAL MINES AND COFFEE GROUNDS

When Mike and Jinny first bought the business, it had only one account. This account, located 60 miles out of town, was the offices of a coal mining operation. Two days a week, while Jinny was at home with the financial books, Mike would drive out to the coal mine and clean the bathrooms and the offices.

The Isaksons had set up the business in the basement of their home. Since finances were tight, they decided not to purchase a desk. Instead, they bought two dented file cabinets and a damaged door from a building materials shop. They put the door over the two cabinets and then placed a piece of glass over it.

Mike remembers those hard first months. "We had been in business for about eight months and were just about out of money, so Jinny had gotten a substitute-teaching job. I felt like we were failing because she had to get that job. So I went downstairs and made a pot of coffee. I was sitting at my desk with the two filing cabinets, and the doorknob hole we used for tossing our trash, and I looked over at the phone, but it never rang. I drank the whole pot of coffee, and then about three hours later, I decided to make more. I threw the old coffee into the trash can and got more water and put it in the percolator. We used a plastic spoon to scoop up the coffee, and when I dug in, I heard it hit bottom. I felt so bad because there wasn't much coffee left, there wasn't much money left, and Jinny had to substitute teach. I decided I had better save that coffee. So I put the coffee back in the can, dug the used grounds out of the garbage, and reperked them. It was the most terrible coffee I ever drank in my life. I was so low, and I seriously wondered if we were going to make it. I remember that feeling of despair. I realized that I had gotten preoccupied getting ready to serve instead of going out and getting customers first. I needed to get out and see adjusters and janitorial accounts and call on retail carpet stores and introduce myself. I just needed to get out and sell."

STINKIN' THINKIN'

As Mike started to focus on selling, the business began to grow, but still he had to fight a tendency to despair. As he considered this propensity, he decided to name it "Stinkin' Thinkin'." For instance, when his pager sounded, usually his first thought was, *There is trouble with an account. Someone is calling in to complain.* Mike soon recognized that 90 percent of the pages were from customers who wanted to give him more business because they were so pleased with the work he was doing.

Mike also had to fight this Stinkin' Thinkin' whenever he picked up the mail. The business had a post office box, and he dreaded seeing the little yellow slips that occasionally appeared in the box since they represented registered letters that might mean that an account was being terminated. "As I waited to claim the registered letter at the post office counter, I would die a million deaths and wonder which client had sent it, why would they cancel the service, I bet it is this one, and so on. I would walk up to the mailbox and turn the key and if I saw a yellow slip in there it would just drive me nuts. When I received a yellow slip on Saturday afternoon, I would have to wait till Monday morning to find out who it was from and what they wanted. I allowed myself to be plagued by questions and doubts."

THE SERVICEMASTER FAMILY GROWS

When the business was in their home, the Isaksons frequently had to get up at night to help the employees returning from their late-night jobs. Mike and Jinny would get up, help put the van and equipment away, and then they would go back to sleep. "It was like having high school kids. 'Okay,' we would say, 'Monty is back now. Here comes Steve. Now we can go to sleep.'"

In the early 1980s Mike hired a young man without really looking at his application. This young man had just finished going through a drug and alcohol rehabilitation program, and when he filled out the application, his sobriety measured only a few days or weeks. During the ten years that Mike employed him, the man became part of the family, and they walked together through many difficulties. Together they buried the employee's six-year-old son, who had died from a brain aneurism. When Mike and Jinny made the move from franchise owner to work for the home office, this employee purchased part of their business. As they were closing the deal, the employee-turned-entrepreneur said, with tears streaming down his face, "Part of the reason that I have maintained sobriety for over ten years is because I've worked for a company like ServiceMaster."

ServiceMaster's four corporate objectives made sense for Mike from the beginning, although at first the objective *Honoring God in all we do* was intimidating. "I was afraid that people would hold me accountable for that. I feared that they would throw it back in my face and say, 'What you just did didn't honor God.' I admit that I didn't want that accountability at the beginning. Then I began to understand how wonderful accountability is. I learned that there was a standard for the way I conducted myself and ran my business. For me, that standard was defined in my personal relationship with Jesus Christ. I don't insist that others believe what I believe. It's just that we need to understand that there is an absolute authority for the way we conduct ourselves and our businesses."

EATING WITH THE FAMILY

Mike and Jinny caught a vision for what could happen in their business when they attended their first national convention in 1978, in Chicago. We watched our peers walk across the stage to receive awards and we looked at each other and said, "We want to win."

Even today, Mike can't overestimate the value of attending ServiceMaster's conferences. Aside from inspiring them to win awards, the conferences afforded them the opportunity to be associated with winning business owners. It was a platform for them to get to know successful franchisees and to learn, firsthand, how they were growing their business. It changed their perspective. It was then they learned that they couldn't afford to miss the conferences, which Mike soon called, "Eating with the family."

"The conferences were an opportunity for us to push back from our business and learn how to make it better. Associating with other owners at the conferences helped us to see that there is power in the ServiceMaster brand, and that I can have an effect on the entire ServiceMaster system by how I conduct my business. I began to understand just how powerful the ServiceMaster trademark is. I saw how the culture that has been developed over the last 50 years has been lived out. I saw the advantage of networking with people who have years of experience and the benefit of learning from their mistakes and successes. I had the opportunity to interact with very brilliant and successful business people." The Isaksons were quick learners, as is borne out by the fact that they won the Marion E. Wade Master Award in 1980.

TIME FOR FURTHER DEVELOPMENT AND GROWTH

Even though Mike and Jinny's business was successful and had a good cash flow, Mike didn't feel like he was being stretched or challenged enough. His friend Dick Armstrong told him that there was as much danger in comfort as there was in barely hanging on. Mike found himself increasingly less challenged by the business. He enjoyed the opportunity to take a stronger leadership role in the home office. Because of the ServiceMaster corporate objective to help people develop, Mike became the first franchisee to be part of the Idea Review Council. Then he was elected president of the council. It was then, during conversations with people like Brian Oxley, Dick Armstrong, Denis Horsfall, Dan Kellow, Bill Pollard, and others that Mike began to see that there were opportunities to stretch and grow within the ServiceMaster home office.

In 1990, Mike was offered the opportunity to grow in leadership, as he became vice president of market expansion of Merry Maids, a ServiceMaster subsidiary, and moved to Omaha, Nebraska. Although this was a challenge for him, he remembers how Don Parkhurst, the president of Merry Maids, helped him. "This was a man who was absolutely committed to helping me develop," Mike stated emphatically. "He helped me move from being an entrepreneur to becoming part of the home office. He always found time to sit down and visit with me, and talk me through various issues. When I talked with Don, I always felt that there was nothing else in the whole world that was as important to him at that moment as talking with me. He was very patient, an encouraging guy."

In 1993 Mike became the President and Chief Operating Officer of Merry Maids. Mike stayed with Merry Maids for five years and then accepted the position that he now holds as president and chief operating officer of the Franchise Services Group. As he's been stretched and enlarged, he's developed a very specific philosophy about the absolute virtue found in giving other people the opportunity to develop.

PEOPLE ARE MADE TO BE DEVELOPED

"I believe that God made each person a unique individual with specific skills, strengths, and talents. We are created by Him to be stretched and to grow those unique qualities. I believe that the ServiceMaster Clean family is one avenue that God uses to accomplish that goal. We have the opportunity to be part of God's plan as we help challenge and develop others."

Mike recognizes the uniqueness of the opportunities for growth within ServiceMaster. "Jinny and I had some skills and abilities, but if we hadn't been given a chance, we wouldn't have been able to take the next step. We don't have a pedigree or an MBA from Harvard. But we're blessed enough to belong to a company that believes in giving people the opportunity to grow."

"I've personally experienced how the second objective, *Helping people develop,* works. The officers in ServiceMaster understood that I needed more development. They gave me that chance. In the corporate world, and in most franchising businesses, that's a radical notion. You just don't see management going out and recruiting franchisees. Seventy-five percent of the people in key positions of leadership in ServiceMaster are former franchisees. That's very unique in the franchising world. Our whole company is committed to people development, giving people the chance to move on to the next level."

Mike and Jinny realize that their growth as individuals, as parents, and as part of the ServiceMaster organization is due in great measure to the people who have mentored and developed them. This mentoring and development has come at the hands of the people they have been privileged to work with in the ServiceMaster family. The stories of many of these individuals are told in this book. Men like Doug Pound, Jim Wassell, Don Rudge, Bob Groff and Bob McDonell continue to be instrumental in Mike's development.

Mike knows from personal experience the benefits of ServiceMaster's emphasis on helping people develop. This commitment has been part of the fabric of his relationships with former ServiceMaster CEOs, Bill Pollard and Carlos Cantu. He's been amazed at how each of these men have taken a personal interest in his development, not only in his private and professional life, but also in his life as a "man before God." Each of the men he has served under, including his present employer, Ernie Mrozek, President an COO of the ServiceMaster Consumer Services Group, and his former employer, Rob Keith, have been exemplary leaders. They have taken seriously the responsibility for the development of the individuals they have been privileged to direct. This dedicated leadership is an important hallmark of the ServiceMaster Clean commitment to people development and the commitment to corporate objectives.

GROWING PROFITABLY BENEFITS EVERYONE

Mike realizes, as much as anyone else, the importance of giving people the chance to develop. But he also recognizes that in order to pursue that goal, everyone in the organization must pursue growth and, ultimately, profits.

"I used to wonder why ServiceMaster stressed growth so much. *Grow, grow, grow.* Why couldn't we just relax and enjoy the fruits of our labor?

"One day, while I was training our employees in our business, it all made sense. I asked the class, 'What would happen if this business doubled in size?' The class responded, 'There would be more people here.' 'Right,' I responded. 'And if there were more employees here, how would your position in the company change?' 'Maybe I would be a manager,' the employees responded. 'Right,' I said. 'If we don't grow, then our business won't sustain profit, and we aren't going to help other people develop.'

"Sometimes people say that the only reason we want their businesses to grow is so that we can have more fee income. I just tell them that they are right. Without growth, we won't have the chance to build our services and develop people who will help them build their businesses. The beautiful part of franchising is that as the franchises grow, our home office support can grow as well. We all grow together. That is the beauty and power of franchising."

THE FRANCHISEE'S COMPENSATION

Mike sees that every franchisee is compensated in three distinct ways. When he starts his business and begins to take a paycheck home, he's compensated. Secondly, when he decides to sell his business, he's compensated by the equity that he's built. Third, the franchise owner is paid off most significantly in lives that have been changed. "We're paid off when the people we hire as janitorial housekeepers end up buying a franchise. When a secretary is helped to develop so that she becomes a sales manager, we have received compensation. We not only change lives for this world, but we can change lives for eternity. Hopefully, by the way we conduct our business we have given our employees an opportunity to learn more about God. That's the real compensation."

Mike believes that the greatest challenge facing his company is the stewardship of the employees. "We've got to realize our responsibility to provide for them. Not only in their remuneration, but also by providing safe, technically advanced working environments. But the greatest responsibility we have is to care for them as individuals, to be stewards of their God-given potential. If we're doing this, then we won't have problems with retention."

PRINCIPLES, PEOPLE, PERFORMANCE

The road to the future has been plainly mapped out before Mike Isakson. "ServiceMaster is a principled organization," Mike stated. "We honor God in all we do. I believe that if we are a principled organization, then people will stay with us and we will have the opportunity to develop them. As a result of the principles and the people working together in agreement, we will be better able to perform for the customer and provide excellence, which means we will grow more profitable."

As Mike looks out over the horizon toward the future, he does so holding Jinny's hand, just as he has for more than a quarter of a century. Their children, Curtis and Catherine, too, stand looking into the future from the vantage point of having grown up in a ServiceMaster family—a family that believes in helping people grow and mature.

"My father, mother, and each of my brothers and sisters have all been involved in education. I'm the only one that's not a teacher," Mike confessed. Although Mike Isakson might not be working in a local school district, he's just as committed to learning and people development as any teacher who ever picked up chalk and an eraser.

"I'm not so much a teacher," Mike stated humbly, "as I am a learner. I am teaching, but I'm also learning so much from others like Carlos Cantu and Bill Pollard. I believe that God has a plan for me and my family and I trust that He will guide and direct us. His guidance and direction will continue to reach into our business life, and into what we do today and tomorrow, not only in our home but also in this office."

APPENDIX:

IMPORTANT NAMES IN THE
SERVICEMASTER CLEAN FAMILY

Dick Armstrong. Beginning in 1964, Mr. Armstrong served
ServiceMaster Clean in many areas, including Vice President and
General Manager of ServiceMaster International division, Vice
President of East and West divisions of the Hospital division and
Senior Vice President of ServiceMaster Residential/Commercial
Services. Mr. Armstrong also served on the Board of Directors. In
1998 he retired and joined the Armstrong family in their Merry
Maids and ServiceMaster Clean franchises.

Andy Beal. Mr. Beal joined a ServiceMaster Clean franchise in
Denver as a salesman in 1980. Six months later, he bought his
own franchise, and in 1987 bought a ServiceMaster LawnCare
distributorship. He joined ServiceMaster Clean's corporate staff
in 1994 as Commercial Program Director.

Jesse Berthume (deceased). Mr. Berthume joined ServiceMaster
in the late 1940s after being recruited from Minneapolis to
become the corporate carpet cleaning salesman. Mr. Berthume
worked with ServiceMaster of Chicago until he retired in the
1960s. He created the ServiceMaster unit system, as well as forms
for estimating and billing that are still in use today.

Ed Brown (deceased). Mr. Brown owned a ServiceMaster distributor business with Eric Robinson in the mid 1970s. In 1978 he
took a position with ServiceMaster corporate as a regional operations manager. In 1983 he left the corporate office to join a distributor operation in Santa Barbara.

Carlos Cantu. Served as President of Terminix when ServiceMaster acquired Terminix in 1986. Also served as President & CEO of ServiceMaster. He is now semi-retired but continues to serve on the ServiceMaster Board of Directors. Mr. Cantu was instrumental in helping ServiceMaster grow into a large, multi-branded company.

Henry Citchen. Joined ServiceMaster Clean in 1982 as a Contract Services franchise owner in St. Louis, Missouri.

Bernie Cozett. In the early 1950s Mr. Cozett was hired by ServiceMaster as a chemist. He worked as Technical Director and later was heavily involved in the beginnings of SERMAC, an industrial cleaning franchise. He is now retired, spending time fishing and golfing in Florida.

Bob DeJong. Started as a franchisee and distributor in San Francisco. Mr. DeJong then joined the corporate staff where he served in various management positions, including Vice President of Operations. He retired in 1999.

Bill Emberlin. Joined ServiceMaster in 1962, selling carpet cleaning door-to-door. In 1966 he bought a janitorial franchise in Portland and then in 1968 a distributorship which he owned until 1996. He currently owns four franchises in the Portland area.

Bob Fallon (deceased). Served as a franchise owner and distributor beginning in the late 1950s. Mr. Fallon was a partner of John Emmons in Boston.

Cal Flaig. Began his career with ServiceMaster as a corporate employee in the mid 1950s and then served as a franchise owner and distributor in Minneapolis. He is now retired.

Frank Flack. Joined Marion Wade as training and support manager for ServiceMaster in the late 1950s. He is now retired.

Tom Gandee. Served as a regional manager starting in 1975. In 1977 Mr. Gandee became the General Manager of a Washington

D.C. office and then in 1979 purchased a distributorship. After selling his distributorship in 1996, he purchased and is now president of Floor Coverings International. Mr. Gandee was the author and initial promoter of the ServiceMaster QRV program.

Jerry Giesinger. From 1982 to 1995 Mr. Giesinger owned a ServiceMaster franchise in Minot, ND. In 1995 he joined the corporate staff as Director of National Accounts and is now serving as Director of Training for the Academy of Service.

Bob Groff. Became a franchise owner in Grand Forks, ND in 1975. He then joined the corporate staff as a regional/area operations manager in 1978. In 1981 Mr. Groff purchased a distributorship in Seattle and served there until he rejoined the corporate staff in 1994 as Vice President.

Ken Hansen (deceased). In 1946 Mr. Hansen began working behind the scenes with Marion Wade. In 1947 he joined ServiceMaster and pulled the founders together. He was a salesman and financial advisor and led ServiceMaster as CEO. Mr. Hansen never really retired from ServiceMaster.

Harry Heard. In the 1950s Mr. Heard was recruited by Ken Hansen to sell franchises for ServiceMaster.

Chuck Hodgin, Sr. Recruited by Marion Wade in 1946 to serve as helper/crew chief on a cleaning crew for Wade Chemical Company. In 1960 he started his own business, ServiceMaster of Chicago, and is still serving as a franchisee/distributor today.

Denis Horsfall (deceased). Started his career with ServiceMaster as a salesman and then served in various positions, including President and Vice President of ServiceMaster Residential/Commercial Services. He also had a business in San Diego with Gerry Farrelly and a distributorship in Baltimore.

Stan Hunt. Mr. Hunt is known as the "father of Spotlight carpet cleaning" in Canada. He worked in Thane McNeil's business in Toronto in the 1960s and then owned a successful ServiceMaster franchise.

Dan Kellow. Became a ServiceMaster regional marketing coordinator in the Northeast United States in 1977 and then served in various positions, including Vice President of Market Expansion until he retired in 2000.

Lloyd Lenn. Served as a distributor with Myron Clark in the Minneapolis area.

Steve Losorwith. Started with ServiceMaster in 1984 as a franchise owner in Seattle. In 1995 he joined the corporate staff and has served in various positions, including his present position as General Manager and Vice President of Furniture Medic.

Paul Marth. Began his career with ServiceMaster in the mid 1950s as the first distributor, serving Washington D.C. He is now retired.

Thane McNeil. In the early 1950s he started as a helper and crew chief for a ServiceMaster business. He later became a franchisee and distributor in Canada. Mr. McNeil is now retired.

Art Melvin. Mr. Melvin was recruited by Ken Hansen to serve as a franchise recruiter and sales manager.

Alan Moore (deceased). Joined ServiceMaster in 1963 as a franchise owner and then served as a distributor in the mid 1970s.

Ed Morgan. Began his career with ServiceMaster in the early 1950s selling franchises and providing franchise support. He later served as Executive Vice President of Operations for ServiceMaster Res/Com and Management Services.

Gene Nickel. Served as regional manager and financial officer for ServiceMaster beginning in the late 1960s.

Brian Oxley. Mr. Oxley started with ServiceMaster in 1976 and became President in 1990. In 1992 he served as President of International and New Business Development. He later served in various positions with ServiceMaster Management Services and is currently a distributor for ServiceMaster in Japan.

Bill Pollard. Joined ServiceMaster in 1977 and served as Chief Executive Officer from 1983 to 1993 as well as 1999 to 2001. He is the author of *The Soul of the Firm* and has contributed to other books and magazines. Now serves as Chairman of the Board of The ServiceMaster Company.

Dale Stevens (deceased). Served in the late 1960s as a ServiceMaster regional manager.

Bill Sunderland. In the early 1950s Mr. Sunderland started in the rug cleaning business in Baltimore. He later moved to Atlanta and served as a ServiceMaster franchisee and distributor.

Marion Wade (deceased). Mr. Wade founded ServiceMaster in the 1940s and served in many capacities throughout his career, including visionary and counselor.

Bob Wenger (deceased). Once a district carpet representative for Brown & Bigelow in Chicago, Mr. Wenger invested with Marion Wade to form Wade-Wenger Associates, which was the foundation for ServiceMaster.

Ken Wessner (deceased). From a sales manager for Club Aluminum, Mr. Wessner joined Marion Wade and Ken Hansen to help found ServiceMaster. He later led the ServiceMaster Healthcare Division and was also President and Chief Executive Officer.

Warren Wigard. Hired by Marion Wade to sell carpet cleaning in downtown Chicago.

ENDNOTES

"Them That Honor Me, I Will Honor"
The Story of George Meyer, Jr.
1. Marion E. Wade with Glenn D. Kittler, *The Lord Is My Counsel* (Englewood Cliffs, NJ: Prentice-Hall, 1966), p. 167.
2. Wade, *ibid.*

The True Reward: Lifelong Friendships
The Story of John Emmons
1. Marion E. Wade, Glenn D. Kittler, *The Lord Is My Counsel* (Englewood Cliffs, NJ: Prentice-Hall, 1966), p. 100.
2. *Ibid*, p. 94.

"We Are Family"
The Story of the George and Lula Holland Family
1. Marion E. Wade with Glenn D. Kittler, *The Lord Is My Counsel* (Englewood Cliffs, NJ: Prentice-Hall, 1966), p. 23.

Training and Trailblazing
The Story of Gerry Farrelly and Phil Fitzpatrick
1. Marion E. Wade, Glenn D. Kittler, *The Lord Is My Counsel* (Englewood Cliffs, NJ: Prentice-Hall, 1966), p. 100.

Integrity and Individual Achievement: Fulfilling the American Dream
The Story of George and David Albino
1. Marion E. Wade with Glenn D. Kittler, *The Lord Is My Counsel* (Englewood Cliffs, NJ: Prentice-Hall, 1966), p. 56.

The Beloved Tradition
The Story of Bobby and Velma Simmons
1. Marion E. Wade with Glenn D. Kittler, *The Lord Is My Counsel* (Englewood Cliffs, NJ: Prentice-Hall, 1966), p. 62.

Building from the Heart
The Story of Reece and Donna Conner
1. Marion E. Wade with Glenn D. Kittler, *The Lord Is My Counsel* (Englewood Cliffs, NJ: Prentice-Hall, 1966), p. 23.

Standing on the Shoulders of Giants
The Story of Jeff and Julie Strong
1. Marion E. Wade with Glenn D. Kittler, *The Lord Is My Counsel* (Englewood Cliffs, NJ: Prentice-Hall, 1966), p. 32.

Rx: Caregivers
The Story of Skip and Mary Ann Fryling
   1. Pollard, C. William, Chairman of the ServiceMaster Company, *The Soul of the Firm* (Grand Rapids: Zondervan Publishing House, 1996), p. 47.

Realizing the Dream
The Story of Doug and Cathy Pound
   1. Marion E. Wade with Glenn D. Kittler, *The Lord is My Counsel* (Englewood Cliffs, NJ: Prentice-Hall, 1966), p. 129.

Humble Mentors
The Story of Wes and Barb Mitchell
   1. Marion E. Wade with Glenn D. Kittler, *The Lord Is My Counsel* (Englewood Cliffs, NJ: Prentice-Hall, 1966), p. 146.

Genuinely Effective Leaders
The Story of Bob and Claire Knapp
   1. Marion E. Wade with Glenn D. Kittler, *The Lord Is My Counsel* (Englewood Cliffs, NJ: Prentice-Hall, 1966), p. 45.
   2. MacDonald, Gordon, *The Effective Father* (Wheaton, IL: Living Books), 1986.

A Seemingly Insignificant Service
The Story of Bob and Becky Smith
   1. Marion E. Wade, Glenn D. Kittler, *The Lord Is My Counsel* (Englewood Cliffs, NJ: Prentice-Hall, 1966), p. 45.

Teaching Is Your Business
The Story of Ian England
   1. Pollard, C. William, Chairman of the ServiceMaster Company, *The Soul of the Firm* (Grand Rapids: Zondervan Publishing House, 1996), p. 114.

An Affair of the Heart
The Story of Bob and Dee McDonell
   1. Marion E. Wade with Glenn D. Kittler, *The Lord Is My Counsel* (Englewood Cliffs, NJ: Prentice-Hall, 1966), p. 85.

A Team Builder
The Story of Randy McCall
   1. Marion E. Wade, Glenn D. Kittler, *The Lord Is My Counsel* (Englewood Cliffs, NJ: Prentice-Hall, 1966), p. 23.

Plotting Out A Winning Strategy
The Story of Charles A. and Alyce Horton
   1. Marion E. Wade with Glenn D. Kittler, *The Lord Is My Counsel* (Englewood Cliffs, NJ: Prentice-Hall, 1966), p. 31.

"Why Do You Do This?"
The Story of Evelyn Brown
   1. Marion E. Wade with Glenn D. Kittler, *The Lord Is My Counsel* (Englewood Cliffs, NJ: Prentice-Hall, 1966), p. 82.

Stewardship: One Tradition, Four Generations
The Clark Family Story
   1. Marion E. Wade with Glenn D. Kittler, *The Lord Is My Counsel* (Englewood Cliffs, NJ: Prentice-Hall, 1966), p.7.

The People We Touch
The Story of Mike and Jinny Isakson
   1. Marion E. Wade with Glenn D. Kittler, *The Lord Is My Counsel* (Englewood Cliffs, NJ: Prentice-Hall, 1966), p. 131.